THE PRODIGAL
YOU LOVE

THE PRODIGAL YOU LOVE

INVITING LOVED ONES BACK TO THE CHURCH

Theresa Aletheia Noble, FSP

Foreword by Father Dave Dwyer, CSP

Pauline
BOOKS & MEDIA
Boston

Library of Congress Cataloging-in-Publication Data

Noble, Theresa.
The prodigal you love : inviting loved ones back to the church / Theresa Noble, FSP ; foreword by Fr. Dave Dwyer, CSP.
pages cm
ISBN 978-0-8198-6004-0 -- ISBN 0-8198-6004-2
1. Ex-church members--Catholic Church. 2. Non-church-affiliated people. 3. Church work with ex-church members--Catholic Church. 4. Prodigal son (Parable) I. Title.
BX2347.8.E82N63 2014
248'.5--dc23

2014004257

Published by Pauline Books & Media, 50 Saint Pauls Avenue, Boston, MA 02130-3491

Printed in the U.S.A.

www.pauline.org

Pauline Books & Media is the publishing house of the Daughters of St. Paul, an international congregation of women religious serving the Church with the communications media.

1 2 3 4 5 6 7 8 9   18 17 16 15 14

For my parents, Jane and Chris,
who loved and prayed me back to the Church

---◇◆◇---

The Parable of the Prodigal Son

Then Jesus said, "There was a man who had two sons. The younger of them said to his father, 'Father, give me the share of the property that will belong to me.' So he divided his property between them. A few days later the younger son gathered all he had and traveled to a distant country, and there he squandered his property in dissolute living.

"When he had spent everything, a severe famine took place throughout that country, and he began to be in need. So he went and hired himself out to one of the citizens of that country, who sent him to his fields to feed the pigs. He would gladly have filled himself with the pods that the pigs were eating; and no one gave him anything. But when he came to himself he said, 'How many of my father's hired hands have bread enough and to spare, but here I am dying of hunger! I will get up and go to my father, and I will say to him, "Father, I have sinned against heaven and before you; I am no longer worthy to be called your son; treat me like one of your hired hands."'

"So he set off and went to his father. But while he was still far off, his father saw him and was filled with compassion; he ran and

put his arms around him and kissed him. Then the son said to him, 'Father, I have sinned against heaven and before you; I am no longer worthy to be called your son.' But the father said to his slaves, 'Quickly, bring out a robe—the best one—and put it on him; put a ring on his finger and sandals on his feet. And get the fatted calf and kill it, and let us eat and celebrate; for this son of mine was dead and is alive again; he was lost and is found!' And they began to celebrate.

"Now his elder son was in the field; and when he came and approached the house, he heard music and dancing. He called one of the slaves and asked what was going on. He replied, 'Your brother has come, and your father has killed the fatted calf, because he has got him back safe and sound.' Then he became angry and refused to go in. His father came out and began to plead with him. But he answered his father, 'Listen! For all these years I have been working like a slave for you, and I have never disobeyed your command; yet you have never given me even a young goat so that I might celebrate with my friends. But when this son of yours came back, who has devoured your property with prostitutes, you killed the fatted calf for him!'

"Then the father said to him, 'Son, you are always with me, and all that is mine is yours. But we had to celebrate and rejoice, because this brother of yours was dead and has come to life; he was lost and has been found.'"

— LUKE 15: 11–32

Contents

———◇◇◇———

Foreword

Standing in the back of church after Mass, I'm shaking hands with the good People of God as they stream toward the light beyond the doors. Most slow their pace just enough for me to give the briefest of blessings on their upcoming week as I attempt to convey slightly more sincerity than a flight attendant saying, "Bye now." I like to think I'm working an assembly line of grace.

One person in the crowd has a more pointed agenda, however. She stops right in front of me and grasps my hand, while the rest of the congregation re-routes around us as if we were a construction zone during rush hour. With a distressed look on her face, she implores, "Father, please help. . . . My heart is breaking. Please tell me what I can do to get my son to go back to Church." I offer a sympathetic look that strains to express my own and the Church's genuine concern for one of the lost sheep. At the end of a short exchange, I recommend prayer and perseverance, although even to my ears this sounds like a platitude. As the

woman walks away, inevitably unsatisfied with my lack of a solu-
tion, all I can think is, "I really wish that gift shop just behind me
had a book that I could recommend for her—a book that
addresses this pastoral problem well and even lays out the process
of inviting your loved ones back."

The bad news is that this is not an account of one particular
Sunday. Replace the woman's face with a different one, exchange
the word "son" for daughter/grandchild/niece/husband/friend/
loved one, and this scene is repeated in the life of a priest way too
often. Wrestling with this issue goes beyond the clergy, too. It is
not hyperbole to suggest that every adult practicing Catholic has
at least one person in their life who is away from the Church and
the sacraments—a lost sheep who has slowly wandered off, or a
prodigal child who ran away with disdain. In fact, research has
shown that if we were to count all the so-called "former" Catholics
together as a group, they would be the second-largest religious
denomination in the United States, outnumbering even Southern
Baptists. That's a lot of people! How can we get them back? How
can all of us be agents of change?

The good news is that you're holding the book I and so many
others have been waiting for. Finally, I have an answer to, "Father,
what can I do?" We've heard a lot in the Church lately about what
recent popes have called the New Evangelization. Sometimes this
can become a very "churchy" enterprise at the level of diocesan-
wide programs and theological symposia at Catholic universities.
A slightly more "Jesus approach" would be to go about it one on
one, face to face, heart to heart. That's why *The Prodigal You Love:
Inviting Loved Ones Back to the Church* is the New Evangelization
par excellence. Theresa Aletheia Noble, FSP, has given every adult
Catholic a spiritual handbook for loving people (not haranguing
them) back to the community of faith. She reminds us that we are

not only called by Christ to this important mission, we are—all of us—quite capable of carrying it out.

As a Paulist priest, welcoming distant Catholics back to the Church is something very close to my heart, as it is ingrained in us even before we begin our seminary studies. The ministry my brother Paulists have tasked me with at present (www.BustedHalo.com) consists of creatively finding new ways to reach out to young adult Catholics. They're the elusive 18 to 39-year-old crowd who prefer the label "spiritual but not religious." These days most are part of the millennial generation, who, as both faith-based and secular sociologists tell us, eschew identifying with any large institution, particularly church. The stats get more daunting with every published survey. At present, a third of American adults under thirty years old claim no affiliation with any organized religion—a number that has tripled in just a couple of decades. If anything has become clear to me in my ten years in this ministry, it is that we select few who do this for a living (indeed, as our vocation) cannot possibly invite back to the Church the millions of people who are not practicing their faith. We need your help! Selfishly, I see this book as mobilizing a global task-force of New Evangelizers. And now that you're reading this, you are one! But don't be scared: it's really quite simple.

You know who makes it look effortless? Our Holy Father. In a very short time, Pope Francis has shown that we Catholics can be—indeed *need* to be—more charitable, loving and understanding when it comes to engaging people with whom we disagree. He has single-handedly shifted the Church's approach to one that involves taking the Gospel to the streets, meeting people and saying, "I'd really like to hear where you're coming from." Like the pope, Sister Theresa pointedly yet gently reminds us that this process of stirring the flame of faith in the hearts of our loved ones is not all about what's wrong with "them"; it needs to start with each of us, you and me.

Lest I come off sounding too much like a detached, professional clergyman, let me clearly say that I need to read and heed this book as much as anyone. I candidly admit to my own personal pain around my friends and family members who have left the Church. Much like you, it hurts me when people I care deeply about turn away from the beautiful gift of our Catholic faith. Even though I'm a priest, I have definitely felt helpless in certain situations not knowing how best to "work on them" to return. I too need to be reminded that I must allow myself to be conformed more into the likeness of Christ so that my loved ones cannot help but be attracted to the community that gathers around his table.

Pray with me for just a moment. . . . "Lord, in your wisdom and love transform my heart, renew my actions, make gentle my words, and in doing so, draw your children back into your loving embrace and to the community of your Church."

Now I can't wait for the next time someone comes up to me after Mass asking for help with their prodigal loved ones. Help has arrived!

Father Dave Dwyer, CSP

Acknowledgments

Thank you first to my parents who looked upon me with the Father's love and prayed for me unceasingly when I was away from the Church. Thank you Kelly, Michael, Javier, Anthony, Kate, and Joanne for trusting me with your stories. I am very blessed to know you all. Thank you Fr. Anselm, Fr. Anthony, Michael, Lucie, Dan, Ami, Monica, and Sr. Marianne Lorraine Trouvé, FSP, for your feedback in the editing process; your comments and changes were extremely helpful and humbling. Thank you Sr. Jacqueline Jean-Marie Gitonga, FSP; Sr. Khristina Galema, FSP; Sr. Carmen Christi Pompei, FSP; and Erin Nolan for contributing heartfelt prayers for the appendix. Thank you to my sisters in community; my siblings David, Sarah, Elizabeth, Mary Margaret; all my friends; and everyone who prayed for this book and continue to pray for its readers and for all of our loved ones who are away from the Church and far from God. May God draw them near to his merciful heart and use our lives as instruments of his peace and love.

Introduction

If you picked up this book, it is likely that you love someone who is away from the Church, or you might want someone you love to become Catholic. You may think about this reality often, or you may hardly think of it at all. But you picked up this book because something in your heart tells you that you could respond to this situation in a better way.

Even Jesus had a hard time getting through to his friends and family. He lamented this reality in the Gospel of Mark: "Prophets are not without honor, except in their hometown, and among their own kin, and in their own house" (6:4). When Jesus was among friends, relatives, and people he had known his whole life, those who should have known him best, "he could do no deed of power" and "he was amazed at their unbelief" (6:5–6). Perhaps we feel this way with those we love most. We do not understand why they cannot appreciate the gift of Jesus in the Church. We feel powerless to sway them, to move their hearts.

Some might even say that the evangelization of our loved ones, proclaiming or re-proclaiming to them the Good News, is an almost impossible task. This is good. Sometimes we need to face difficult tasks so we can see that all goodness comes from God, not us. It is not by ourselves that we accomplish anything but "through him who strengthens" us (Phil 4:13). Precisely because it is difficult and requires holiness, the evangelization of our loved ones is an intense path to sanctity. The task of evangelizing our friends and family is not for the fainthearted or those weak in faith. It is a hidden work without fanfare or instantaneous results. We work in the knowledge that we may not be successful. Jesus himself was not successful in calling all those he loved to him. But we can be sure that trying is always better, for our loved ones and for us, than not trying at all.

In the Book of Isaiah, we hear the prophetic words that foreshadow the person of Jesus: "a bruised reed he will not break, and a dimly burning wick he will not quench" (42:3). Our loved ones may be bruised, through their own behavior, the behavior of others, or both. The light of their faith may be dimly burning or nonexistent. But we are called to be like Jesus, to tenderly and compassionately guide our loved ones to the healing gaze of the Father and to the burning fire that is his love.

Pope Francis related an incident that reveals one of the most important aspects in evangelizing one's own family and friends. He said:

> I recall the story of a young man, twenty-two years old, who was suffering from a deep depression. [He was a] young man who lived with his mom, who was a widow and who did the laundry of wealthy families. This young man no longer went to work and lived in an alcoholic haze. The mom was not able to help him: every morning before leaving she would simply look at him with great tenderness. Today this young man has a position of

responsibility: he overcame that problem, because in the end that look of tenderness from his mom shook him up. We have to recapture that tenderness, including maternal tenderness.[1]

Take a moment to imagine the loved ones you had in mind when you picked up this book. Picture their smiles, their laughs, and the goodness you know is in their hearts. Perhaps you can remember times in their lives when they were devoted to the faith. You may have recent memories, moments of hope, when it seemed your loved ones might have thought about returning to the Church. Imagine them now back in the Church, sitting in the pews, receiving the sacraments, praying, in strong relationship with God.

Visualize who your loved ones can be, who they were when they were only imagined in the mind of God at the beginning of creation. Hold your loved ones in your mind with a gaze of tenderness, a gaze that sees not their flaws, their sins nor failures, but who they are when they are at their best, who they are deep down inside. Look at them with deep love and recognition; see the person God made each to be. This is the gaze that can change our loved ones, because it is the gaze of God. With this tender gaze of the Father upon his wayward children, we can lead our loved ones back to the Church. It is possible. Come with me on a journey to find out how.

CHAPTER ONE

A Story of Hope

"The wind blows where it chooses, and you hear the sound of it, but you do not know where it comes from or where it goes. So it is with everyone who is born of the Spirit."

— John 3:8

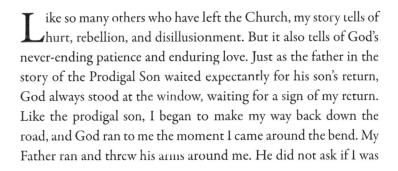

Like so many others who have left the Church, my story tells of hurt, rebellion, and disillusionment. But it also tells of God's never-ending patience and enduring love. Just as the father in the story of the Prodigal Son waited expectantly for his son's return, God always stood at the window, waiting for a sign of my return. Like the prodigal son, I began to make my way back down the road, and God ran to me the moment I came around the bend. My Father ran and threw his arms around me. He did not ask if I was truly sorry, or if I would leave him again. He asked no questions. Instead, he welcomed me, gave me the finest robe, and put a ring on my finger. This story of return to the Father is the story of us all, of you, of me, and of your loved ones. I tell you my prodigal story so that you may see hope for your loved ones in it. The details may differ, but I pray that, like me, your loved ones will choose to begin their journey back to their Father's home, where God is waiting to run to meet them.

My Story

When I was a child, I loved God with all my heart. My devout parents centered our family life on the Catholic faith. The liturgical rhythm of the Church was the heartbeat of our family. My father was a professor who led an evangelism program at a Catholic university. From a young age, I shared my father's enthusiasm for evangelization. When I was only eight years old, I coaxed him into allowing me to attend one of his evangelism classes. Much to the amusement of the students, I filled out the workbook and contributed with gusto. I participated in door-to-door evangelization with my father and handed out religious tracts downtown. Although my interest pleased my father, I did none of this under pressure; a real fire burned in my heart. My fiery faith was authentic, but not yet strong enough to withstand the powerful dousing effect of suffering and cold logic.

Despite my youthful fervor, I was always a natural doubter. When I was about five I doubted the existence of God for the first time. As I climbed the stairs to the second floor of my family's house, suddenly, like a snake pouncing, a thought stung my mind: "What if God doesn't exist?" I felt as if the walls of my secure, warm home had fallen, and I was surrounded by an empty blur of white, the shrill stillness whistling in my ears. I dismissed the thought almost immediately, but the doubt remained, dormant, like a sleeping volcano under the deceptively calm surface of my soul.

Over time my doubts about the existence of God began to resurface as the pounding rain of life's suffering gradually broke down my strong faith. Unfortunately, most of my family's challenges involved people and organizations tied to the Church. My father's career as a theologian was primarily dedicated to evangelization and serving the Church. However, several difficult situations arose, both in his teaching post at a Catholic university and then in his work as the director of religious education in another diocese. My father began working for a secular college. He did not want to stop serving the Church, but all too common politics and divisiveness led him to do so. In the midst of all this, I unfortunately saw some Catholics, including priests and religious, acting in some very un-Christ-like ways. I was a sensitive and impressionable child, and these experiences scandalized me and served to push me further from the faith.

All these things, combined with other family difficulties and topped with the drama of teenage angst, stirred up the perfect storm within me. At fourteen years old, shaking my fist at God, I left the Catholic Church. My parents, thinking this was only a phase, forced me to go to Mass on Sunday. But I was finished. In my heart I had left the Church. I absolutely refused to be confirmed, and when my parents brought it up, I angrily asked them if they really wanted to force me to receive the sacrament. I insisted they would have to drag me to church if they wanted me to be confirmed. I was angry, and I trusted no one. The hypocrisy I had seen among Christians convinced me that it was possible to be a good person without God. I decided to set off on my own.

The faith my parents had carefully and painstakingly instilled in me since childhood quickly dissolved. For reasons that will become clearer later in the book, my formerly strong childhood connection with God, left unused, eventually broke off completely. I became an atheist. Idealistic, nonconformist, and full of anger, I quickly entered the teenage subculture with which I could most identify: I became a punk. Through a friend at my high school, I started to go to punk rock shows and sneak out at night. I chopped off my long hair and started dying it: pink, dark red, platinum blond, anything but normal. I left behind big floppy hats and floral prints for safety pins, chains, and anarchy symbols. I maintained my place on the honor roll, which kept most of my illicit activities unnoticed, but at the same time, a dark world began to absorb me. Before my parents knew it, I had changed from a quiet bookworm into a troubled, angry, and brooding teenager.

At the end of high school, I was accepted into an elite women's college on the East Coast. I was thrilled. This fit my self-image as an intelligent, urbane atheist who would show the world that being a good person did not require imaginary gods. I left the punk rock culture behind; I figured the drug use and related risks would hinder me from making something of myself. Of course, I continued some dangerous behavior, just not enough to get caught in the undertow. But I still wanted to live in rebellion against the status quo, so I lived to separate myself. I listened to obscure indie music, read existentialist philosophy, became active in various causes, and ate only vegan food.

During this unlikely time, without even knowing it, my angry heart began looking for God again. It started with a conversation about miracles. One day a friend and I were sitting on a stone wall, swinging our feet and chatting about transcendent things. I casually said that I believed in miracles. My friend said, "Oh, you mean amazing things that science can explain?" "Of course not," I said. "If something can be explained, it's not miraculous." My friend aptly pointed out that atheists do not usually believe in miracles. "I know," I grumbled. If I believed in miracles, then they had to have a logical cause. "What could cause a miracle?" I thought. At this point I had rejected God for so long that I didn't even think of him as a possible explanation.

My natural attraction to the supernatural led me to look for answers. Like many seekers, I chose the religion furthest from my own. I began reading Buddhist texts and taking philosophy classes on Eastern spiritual thinking. It fascinated me. My exploration of Buddhism helped me begin to accept mystery and paradox. At one point I went to hear a Buddhist monk speak at my college. In some way, his words made me feel as if I were lifted out of my ordinary life. "Desire is the source of suffering"—it sounded so easy and yet so difficult! I began to become open to a deeper reality present in the world than what is readily apparent.

My college was originally Quaker and was near a meeting house so, out of curiosity, I started to also explore the Quaker faith. I began to occasionally attend Quaker meetings (a weekly worship service). The Quakers provided me with a non-dogmatic setting (I would not have accepted anything else) in which I began to explore spirituality again. In that simple wooden building, people gathered for an hour in silence. During the meeting, individuals would stand when they felt they had a message to share. In that pregnant, peaceful, and silent atmosphere, without being aware of it, I began to explore the long silence that had become a wall between God and me.

After college, as part of my independent quest to be a good person and help people, I joined Teach for America, an organization that places college leaders in low-income inner-city and rural schools around the country. The summer after my graduation I was trained in Los Angeles and then was sent to teach a third grade class in Miami. On the first day of school, all of twenty-one years old, I sat behind my desk wide-eyed and anxious, waiting for my students to arrive. The thought of the awesome responsibility before me filled my heart with fear. If I did not do a good job, I feared that my students would leave my classroom more disadvantaged than ever. Most of them had already fallen behind academically. For the first time in my life, I faced a situation I doubted I could handle.

The first month, I went home every day, threw myself on my bed, and cried. Not one of my students could read at grade-level, if at all. By the end of the year, they would need to pass a standardized reading test to move on to the fourth grade. Many of the kids had serious behavior problems. Their difficulties at home, the violence they were exposed to, and the sad family situations they faced continually shocked and saddened me. I began to search desperately for something that would help me keep my head above water. I realized that in order to help my students, I needed to mature and grow as a person.

Looking for something that would bring me peace, I tried meditation. I failed miserably. I would sit cross-legged on my pillow, nodding off to sleep, wondering, "Is this supposed to be so boring? What am I doing wrong?" Every morning I would practice yoga, trying to focus my mind. During lunch breaks I sat outside, looked at the bright clouds, and took deep breaths, counting the hours left in the day. I also started to attend Quaker meetings every Sunday. There I found a supportive community of very kind, highly-educated people, some of whom seemed as unsure about the existence of God as I was. I felt at home. I still did not profess a belief in God, but these spiritual practices soothed my spirit, and the Quaker community offered support and helped keep me afloat.

After I finished teaching, I took some time off and moved to California with my boyfriend, who was studying for his PhD. I applied to law school and envisioned getting into a top school and changing the world. I lived on the campus of the university where my boyfriend was studying. I was surrounded by successful people and the prospect of my own success, but I began to feel like something was not right. My sensitive heart gradually became aware of what felt like a deep chasm in my soul. Something was wrong, very wrong. But I felt deeply confused because on the outside everything seemed so right. So many people would have wanted my life.

Yet, I was not happy. One day as I sat outside my apartment under a tree, tears rolled down my cheeks. I was deeply sad but I didn't know why. I rubbed the top of my hand back and forth against the rough bark of the tree until my skin was red and raw. I wanted my interior pain to be seen exteriorly. Otherwise, I felt as if I would go crazy. Anyone would have said my life was perfect. Yet, I experienced an emptiness that nothing around me could fill. Why was I so unhappy? What was this pain that seemed to rip me apart from the inside out? What was this terrible emptiness?

I had time before I would start law school in the fall, so I decided to take a trip by myself to Costa Rica. A local family hosted me while I worked at a nearby ranch, weeding the garden, carrying firewood, and cooking. Rural life suited me. The spartan living conditions and manual labor were actually a great relief. I felt liberated, free from the complications of life in the United States. I realized how differently most of the world lived from the affluent world into which I was lucky enough to have been born. Health insurance, stocks, retirement, savings, all the things that consume a post-college graduate's plans, didn't matter in this rural town. Yet the people had enough and they were happy. In fact, they were happier, with much less, than most of the people I knew back home. The anxiety I felt almost every day in my normal life melted away. I was at peace here working with my hands and living day to day.

I quickly noticed that almost every person I met in the small town where I lived believed in God. Even if they did not go to church, the existence of God was a given. At first, I tried convincing myself that they were just too uneducated to understand that God was an idea that intelligent people naturally moved beyond. But this mental tactic did not work for long. I realized that in many ways these people were much more mature and intelligent than I was. Perhaps they had not read Kant or Hegel, but they knew life. When I would spout off the freethinking, Western opinions of a spoiled American, my new friends would give me amused but patient looks. At first I felt indignant and embarrassed at their reaction, but I gradually began to realize my own immaturity. These people, who worked hard every day of their lives and believed in God with ease, knew more about life than I did with my many years of expensive education.

Arabela, the mother of the family I stayed with, was a strong Catholic. Every week she would walk with her two daughters to clean the church. It was a poor, concrete building with crumbling walls, but the people of the town painstakingly cared for it. Mass was only celebrated once every two weeks due to a shortage of priests and the rural location of the village. Every other Thursday, small groups of older women would make their way to Mass. Much to my surprise, when I first noticed the little groups of old ladies walking to Mass in the crisp morning air, I felt a pull to join them, but I ignored the feeling wondering if I was going crazy.

One day I felt the pull so strongly that I grit my teeth while working in the garden, trying to resist the feeling with all my strength. Then, for some reason, something inside of me gave and I surrendered. I dropped my hoe and walked to the church. The other volunteers at the ranch where I worked watched me strangely. I could feel their eyes on my back. As I approached the door of the church, conversation died down abruptly. The women waiting for Mass eyed me with suspicion and mild disgust. I was not welcome; I was a foreigner, and a badly behaved one at that! But then Arabela arrived; seeing me, she looked shocked, but a smile quickly broke over her face and she waved me over.

The presider was a city priest from the capital of San Jose. He was fluent in English and was delighted to see a foreigner attending Mass. He spoke slowly during the liturgy so that I could understand, and he would insert little stories and jokes in his homilies that seemed to be for my benefit. I started to go to the church whenever Mass was celebrated. Each time, the other women would give me dagger-like looks. But the priest was always happy to see me, despite the disapproval of most of the other church-goers. With a warm smile, he would reach out his hand to shake mine, and Arabela would pat the seat next to her.

One day after Mass, I went to the local *pulpería*, a tiny grocery store that also served as the bar for the small town. I was talking to some of the locals when the priest approached the *pulpería* with a bright smile. All of the people at the bar sitting on the three rough-hewn wooden benches turned and looked at him with discomfort. He was getting some of the same looks I got when I went to Mass. For me, it was a clash of two worlds. I wondered if the priest would know that I was a fake, that I spent more time at the local bar than I ever did praying. Would he ask me to stop attending Mass?

He ordered a soda in a loud voice and joked with the guy behind the bar. Then he sat down next to me and struck up a conversation. I was impressed by how happy he seemed. We talked about various things while the non-churchgoers at the bar watched us warily. Then, for some reason, I asked him why he had decided to become a priest. "I was a very successful lawyer working for a large corporation," he told me. "I had a beautiful fiancé," he said, and his eyes got a faraway look for a moment. "My life was perfect, but I felt something in my heart, something that was not right. Then I started to pray more and I realized that God was calling me to the priesthood. And how could I say no?" he said with a twinkle in his eye, looking at me as if he just knew I would understand.

I did not understand. It sounded crazy. But something stirred in my heart, and for a moment I considered my life, which, even though I was not practicing my faith, was quite similar. I planned to attend law school in the fall. I assumed I would eventually marry my wonderful boyfriend. Yet something did not feel right. As for the priest, I couldn't understand how someone could be so joyful about leaving behind success and happiness with a family. It seemed quite insane, yet I couldn't deny that this man radiated joy. I left the conversation feeling unsettled. I felt so above Catholicism, and yet this priest—an educated, intelligent, and successful person—had given up everything that I was planning for—because of God. I wondered how he could even be sure God existed. Little did I know that in just a few days I would begin to understand.

One day, early in the morning, I was walking from my host family's house to the ranch where I worked. I looked out at the mountains surrounding me and admired the beauty of the rolling green hills. I could hear the birds singing joyfully. I was filled with gratitude for the day, the mountains, the birds, and the trees rustling gently in the breeze. Unlike back at home, everything felt just right. My soul suddenly swelled, as if it could not contain my gratitude any longer. At that moment, a great wind tore through the trees around me. I felt frightened at its intensity, and the trees seemed to shake for fear with me.

Suddenly a conviction filled me: God exists! I could feel his presence in a way I had not felt since I was a child. And the God who was introducing himself to me was not some sort of universal spirit or sci-fi force that impersonally ran the universe (all ideas I had entertained). I knew in my heart that God was a Person, that he had feelings and desires, and that he loved me in a deep and intimate way. His presence was so much greater than I was; his overwhelming immensity almost stopped my breathing. Yet this love waited to envelop me, waited for my permission. I knew I could not resist him any longer. I surrendered.

Immediately, I knew my life would change. While flying home from Costa Rica, I decided not to go to law school and also to break up with my boyfriend. It was time for a new beginning. I did not quite know why. But I did feel that it would be better for me, better for everyone. God knew why and that satisfied me. I still did not consider myself a Catholic. I continued with my former way of living. Outwardly, not much changed. Another year would pass before I started returning regularly to Mass, and yet another before I was confirmed. Most people around me would not have known anything had changed. Seeds of grace tend to unfold silently before they bloom.

Several months after returning from Costa Rica, I was still living a carefree life. I told myself I had to wait for God to make clear what he wanted for me, but not knowing exactly how that worked, I also made my own plans. I worked at a temporary job, saving up for another trip to Latin America. I dated various men and eventually became involved with one who had been raised Catholic. He still attended Mass occasionally but did not live his faith seriously. However, for the first time, someone close to me—other than my family—saw Catholicism as a good. Even though he did not live it well himself, I could tell that deep down inside he wanted to. One day we were discussing religion and I said something to suggest that I considered myself Catholic. He looked at me in amusement and exclaimed, "You're not Catholic!" I paused briefly, and in a voice that I hardly recognized as my own, the unexpected words came out, "Yes, I am."

I am a person of all or nothing. The moment those words came out of my mouth, things changed. It still took time for God's purifying action to cleanse me of many outward inconsistencies (in fact, God will always be working on these inconsistencies). But interiorly, the inspired words that escaped my mouth that day became the basis for a new will to change my life. To my boyfriend's surprise, I soon grew more serious about the faith than he was. The relationship quickly ended. God was jealously guarding and guiding me. Even when I deviated from his path, he used it for my good, and patiently continued to move me forward, as long as I was willing to follow.

I joined a nearby church in my neighborhood and began attending regularly. The parish community was diverse and full of life. I found supportive friends who helped me to order my life around God and his plans for me rather than my own. I never expected to be back in the Catholic Church, but now I knew that God had unmistakably led me to where I was; I could not deny it. Although I still had many doubts and issues with the Church, the knowledge that God led me to where I was made me feel secure in my doubt. I soon began a program to become confirmed. And just like that, I picked up the thread I had so disdainfully thrown away when I refused the sacrament as an angry fourteen-year-old.

Throughout the Confirmation process, I wrestled with my doubts and all that kept me from the Church for so many years. I could feel the Spirit moving in my life, helping me to understand and accept the faith. I did not suddenly find the answers to all my questions, but I did grow enough to become comfortable with mystery. I began to trust God more and to accept both the joys and the mess of Christian community. The day I was confirmed, I felt as if my soul had found its place again, and the emptiness that had haunted me for so long began to be filled to overflowing.

I wrote this poem to describe what I felt the day the holy oil was placed on my forehead at Confirmation:

I can feel the Spirit sinking into my soul,
I breathe deeply
My pores widen
The Spirit, like the oil, sinks into my being
Making Himself a home.
He finds the fire of my Baptism,
It is ablaze.
He immerses Himself in it,
Melding to me,
His name a seal upon my heart.
It is a moment in time,
But outside of time it stretches on.
I am home.

CHAPTER TWO

The Foundation of Humility

"No one reaches the kingdom of Heaven except by humility."[1]

— Saint Augustine

———◇———

W hen I lived for several months in Costa Rica, I spent most of my days outside, working under the sun. One day before my conversion, I was in the garden tending some basil plants when one of the local farmers stopped by. He said, "Thank God for this day—right Teresita?" I blinked up at him in the bright sun. He looked so pleased that he was sharing this moment with me that I did not want to disappoint him. But I am not one to lie, so I said honestly, "Chepo, I don't believe in God so I don't have anyone to thank." His eyes widened in surprise. He was not peeved by my admission; I saw only compassion and mirth in his eyes. He did not say much in response; he only sighed and shifted his feet. "I see, I see. You had that smile. . . ." He trailed off. I assured him that I could be happy without God and he looked at me again with gentle amusement, his eyes so deep, wise, and expressive that I felt like some primordial being was gazing at me. In that moment, I wanted to connect with him. I wanted to understand the source of his serenity, but all I could do was look up at him, squinting in the sun.

My conversion pivoted around many small moments like this, which shifted and changed my narrow perspective on life, on God, and on the Church. In these moments, other people helped me to look gradually beyond myself and realize that I could find meaning only in my Creator. Most often, the people who successfully pierced my self-assurance and urged me to reconsider my beliefs did so not with complicated arguments but with humility and simplicity.

Humility is absolutely essential in our relationships with loved ones who are away from the Church. If we do not understand the importance of humility, then chances are we will hurt rather than help the likelihood of our loved ones' return to the Church.

Why is humility particularly important in interactions with loved ones who are not practicing their faith? First of all, because humility is the virtue our loved ones need in order to return. Faith begins with humility. In the encyclical *Light of Faith (Lumen Fidei)*, Pope Francis writes: "Faith is God's free gift, which calls for humility."[2] The journey of faith is a process in which one's perspective in life increasingly shifts away from self and toward God. If we do not model humility, then we do little to encourage an attitude of faith in our loved ones. (This is an important point that I will return to later in the chapter.)

Secondly, humility is also important because if we are not humble, we can easily fall into the trap of thinking that we are responsible for another person's return to the Church. This attitude is perhaps among the most dangerous, and can lead to serious missteps that push people away. In order to really live in a compelling way that leads others to faith, we have to give up any savior-complex we might have. What we say and do is not going to save anyone. We have a Savior and his name is Jesus. In order to make any difference in our loved ones' lives, we have to let go of any self-centeredness in our desire for someone to return to the Church.

Because humility is foundational and essential in our relationships with others, we will spend some time exploring this virtue. If we learn to understand the value of humility and allow this virtue to grow in our own lives, then we can interact respectfully with our loved ones. When we act humbly, we can be confident that we are communicating with our loved ones as God communicates with us.

Getting Our Toes Dirty

So, what does humility look like? Humility is a virtue that is not afraid to play in the dirt. The very word derives from the Latin word for dirt or soil, *humus*. Humility has her head in the clouds, close to God, and her bare toes in the mud. Humility speaks regularly to God, as one would with a friend. But she also sees clearly that God is beyond human understanding. Those who possess the virtue of humility see the vast distance between human and Creator. Hence the dirty toes. Everything that separates us from God grounds us in the dirt and covers our toes in mud. Everyone has dirty toes; the humble person is just aware of it.

Those who are humble know that we can only become holy by opening our hearts to God's grace. We do not become holy through our own efforts. We do nothing more than open our hearts. This itself is a grace. And no matter where we are in life, there is always room to open our hearts even more to God. It is easy to lose perspective and think that because we attend Mass and pray regularly, we are somehow better than a person who does not. God may, however, judge the heart of someone who seems far from him to be purer than our own. God has night vision glasses, and a killer aerial view. Time spent with God in prayer leads to the inevitable realization that God does not see things the way we do; he sees much more. If we are humble, we realize that, as human beings, we pretty much have the perspective of an ant compared to God: "For as the heavens are higher than the earth, so are my ways higher than your ways, and my thoughts than your thoughts" (Is 55:9).

When we are humble, we ultimately realize that any failures we experience in relating to our loved ones can be overcome by God, who is so much greater than our failures. We also realize that any success we have in bringing our loved ones closer to God is pure grace. Humility puts things in perspective.

The Humility of Jesus

In his parables, Jesus was fond of using metaphors inspired by nature and the world around him. His audience most likely appreciated this because they were salt of the earth people, the blue-collar workers of his day. Jesus met people where they were. Even when his message was difficult to understand, Jesus spoke with a humble simplicity. He did not use inaccessible language or difficult words. Jesus adapted his approach to each person he met, while at the same time always speaking plainly and clearly. There were times when Jesus spoke with anger and divine authority, and other times when he spoke with gentle frankness. But he always spoke simply.

Seventeenth-century mathematician and philosopher Blaise Pascal affirmed:

> Jesus Christ said great things so simply that it seems as though he had not thought them great; and yet so clearly that we easily see what he thought of them. This clearness, joined to this simplicity, is wonderful.[3]

Why did Jesus choose this style of communication? He must have known that the best way to speak of the things of heaven is with simplicity. We, too, can imitate Jesus and keep things simple. We do not have to be simplistic in sharing the faith, but we can stay on the road of simplicity that gets to the heart of the matter. In the end, if our conversations do not lead our loved ones to a relationship with God, they will not be fruitful.

The way Jesus communicated tells us something of the humility of God. Simplicity is a sign that someone is not focused on him or herself but on the truth. Jesus chose to communicate the Father and nothing else. To desire to be humble is to desire to be like Jesus who lived in constant surrender to the Father. Our surrender to God communicates itself in the beauty of humble simplicity, the fruit of uniting our will completely with God's. This all sounds straightforward, but, in reality, it is not easy to allow God to eclipse our human desire to run our own lives and focus on ourselves. It is not easy to surrender to God in humility. But because God created our hearts, we can be confident that living in union with him will lead to a life that is more in touch with our true desires. And when we live according to our deepest desires, we draw others to seek this union with God that leads to joy.

Saint Paul reminds us of the humility of Christ when he wrote in his letter to the Philippians:

> Let the same mind be in you that was in Christ Jesus, who, though he was in the form of God, did not regard equality with

God as something to be exploited, but emptied himself, taking the form of a slave, being born in human likeness. And being found in human form, he humbled himself and became obedient to the point of death—even death on a cross. (Phil 2:5–8)

Though he was God, Jesus emptied himself. The Greek word Paul uses is *kenóō*, which means "to empty," but the word *kenóō* can also refer to the waning of the moon. The image of the waning moon helps explain what Paul meant by saying Jesus "emptied himself." The moon waxes and wanes, but it never loses anything of itself. A crescent moon is still a full moon; it is just not completely visible to the human eye. When the moon becomes full, it simply reflects fully the light of the sun, but its fullness never changes. In the same way, Jesus remained fully divine when he became human. However, he gave up the dazzling light of his divinity in order to embrace the lowliness of human nature.

Paul continues:

Therefore God also highly exalted him and gave him the name that is above every name, so that at the name of Jesus every knee should bend, in heaven and on earth and under the earth, and every tongue should confess that Jesus Christ is Lord, to the glory of God the Father. (Phil 2:9–11)

Through his death, resurrection, and ascension, Jesus was exalted and brought our humanity closer to the dazzling light of the Divine in order to restore us to our original dignity. What humanity lost through the sin of Adam and Eve, Jesus returned to us. But God, who is never outdone in generosity, did not stop there. We not only received what we had lost, but God has given us even more. This is why at the Easter Vigil we sing, "O happy fault, O necessary sin of Adam, which gained for us so great a Redeemer!" Things are actually *better* for us than if Adam and Eve had never tasted the forbidden fruit.

It is possible to desire to be truly humble like God because Jesus made it possible. By emptying himself and becoming man, Jesus restored humanity's original dignity and gave us the opportunity to become more like him. In the Second Letter of Peter, we are told that we will be able to "become participants of the divine nature" (2 Pt 1:4). The early Church Fathers spoke of this heavenly possibility as "divinization." Saint Athanasius put it succinctly: "God became man so that man might become a god."[4] This is how good God has been to us. Through the sin of Adam, we gained Jesus. The grace that Adam and Eve lost has been restored. Satan tempted Eve in the Garden of Eden with the words: "You will be like God" (Gen 3:5). This was a lie. Without relying on God and obeying him, Adam and Eve lost the chance to become like God. Through Jesus, we have regained this gift.

If we truly believe that we have been given the grace to become like Jesus, then we can grow in the spiritual life by leaps and bounds. And the more we become like Jesus, the more we are like a window drawing others to God, the source of light that streams through us.

Why Humility?

Saint Augustine, one of the greatest converts in Church history, believed humility was a foundational virtue: "Do you wish to rise? Begin by descending. You plan to build a tower that will pierce the clouds? Lay first the foundation of humility." Saint Thomas Aquinas did not believe humility to be the greatest of virtues, but, like Saint Augustine, he held humility to be foundational. Aquinas described humility as the virtue that removes obstacles to other virtues.[5] Seems appropriate, right? Even as a virtue humility takes a humble place in the background, setting the stage for other virtues.

When we engage with someone who is away from the Church, it is important that our encounter help his or her faith to grow, whether it is faith in God or, if the person already believes in God, faith that Jesus instituted the Catholic Church. If the virtue of faith is like a tree that needs to be planted, then it is necessary to first remove the weeds and rocks from the dirt. Aquinas tells us that humility is the virtue that will do just that. Humility rolls up her sleeves and gets dirt under her fingernails as she clears the ground, making the soil ready for the fragile tree of faith. This is why humility, although not necessarily the "greatest" virtue, is nonetheless foundational and absolutely essential when we engage with our loved ones.

Humility is not only necessary for our loved ones to grow in faith, but it is also just as necessary for us. Why? Because in a dialogue, we often look to the person we are communicating with for a cue as to how we should respond. Imagine you are sitting on your couch one Saturday afternoon reading a delightful book and basking in the noonday sun streaming through your window. Suddenly, a friend barges through your door and demands in a loud, accusatory tone, "Why are you just sitting there? If you want to go to the farmers' market, we should leave soon. It's going to close!" Even if you had wanted to go to the farmers' market, the abrupt entrance and your friend's aggression might make you feel attacked. So you shut down and say, "I'm not going!" with as much force as you can muster, and you go back to reading your book.

How we approach a person often determines how he or she will respond. If we approach a person with humility, the person will often respond in that manner. However, if we approach a person aggressively or with self-righteousness, that person will likely respond in the same way and flee from the conversation as soon as possible. A seedling of faith cannot be planted among rocks and thorns. If we take the path of humility, we may elicit humility in the person we approach, clearing aside debris and laying the foundation for faith. Pope Francis emphasizes this lesson when he says that Christians should proclaim the Gospel message in such a way that it will be received, not refused. The Good News deserves to be packaged in a way that reflects the goodness of the news we share. It also deserves to be delivered in a way that makes it more likely to be accepted. Humility answers both of these concerns; it reflects the goodness and simplicity of God, and it makes our message more likely to be received.

It is not just good strategy to be humble in our interactions; it is also part of our call as Christians. Saint Paul writes to the Colossians: "As God's chosen ones, holy and beloved, clothe yourselves with compassion, kindness, humility, meekness, and patience" (Col 3:12). Paul encourages us as Christians to shed what is not of Christ and to clothe ourselves in him. So often in our interactions we do the opposite. We clothe ourselves with carefully constructed masks of pride and other defenses, rather than with humility and meekness. We cling to a self of our own making, and, unfortunately, the selves we construct are often more like tyrannical gods than humans. In the end, to become humble means to shed our self-constructed disguises and embrace who we really are, the beautiful and the not so beautiful. We do this because we cannot embrace God, who is Truth, if we are busy lying and pretending we are something we are not.

In Christian spirituality we often speak of growing in humility as "dying to ourselves." This is not a pleasant sounding phrase, but the meaning behind it is much more beautiful than it sounds. Humility is certainly a dying to oneself, but we die to our *false* selves when we grow in humility. It is our phony constructions of self, our own ideas of what is important, and our careful plans that we leave behind when we die to ourselves. Only when we leave these things behind can we open ourselves to discover who we are meant to be in God. It is only in dying and in emptying ourselves of all that is not from God that we can be filled with God.

Dying to our false self is important independent of whether or not it helps us communicate with loved ones. Growing in humility is a key part of the spiritual journey. But our desire for loved ones to come back to the Church gives new urgency to our need for humility. We need to become humble because our false selves do not know how to evangelize; they are too busy focusing on themselves! If we want to successfully invite others to return to the Church, it is necessary to show them what our faith has done for us. After all, if practicing our faith has not led us to give up our disguises, our idols, and our falseness, then our loved ones will wonder why they should return to a Church whose members behave just like everyone else!

Growing in Humility

It's fairly easy to see the value of humility, but much more difficult to actually become humble. Growing in humility is a lifelong journey. Thankfully, we do not have to attain perfect humility before we share our faith. The work of evangelization is the work of the Holy Spirit. If we depend on the Holy Spirit to guide our words, we can be sure that the Spirit will help us communicate in a humble manner, even if we have not yet mastered the virtue of humility. However, while we certainly need to depend on the Holy Spirit for help, we also should not expect to become humble overnight without any effort. Becoming humble involves struggle; we can work on growing in this virtue in the following ways:

Pray for Humility

The first step to humility is to realize that it is not possible to attain humility without prayer. We cannot skip this first step if we genuinely want to grow in humility. Of course, asking God for humility is probably the appeal that you—and every other sensible person—least desires to make. If you have prayed for humility before, you probably know that God swiftly answers this request with opportunities to exercise the virtue. But many of us do not particularly want to practice humility, as it can be painful to accept opportunities to become smaller, less self-important, less noticed, and less admired.

As we pray for humility, we learn that we are not meant to be the center of our lives. God gradually helps us to remove our false feelings of superiority and our sense of being entitled to special treatment from others. As God answers our prayers, he helps us to see the many ways in which we are attached to a certain view of ourselves. We like to believe that we deserve the easier task, the bigger slice of cake, the flattering comment, and the praise of others. Or, if we tend to the opposite extreme, we may think that we are worthless, ugly, and no good. We are consumed with how we don't measure up. Either way we are wrapped up in ourselves. The truth lies in neither of these realities, so we pray for God to lead us to the truth.

We can be confident that when we ask for humility, God will answer our prayers. Jesus tells us in the Gospel of Matthew:

> Ask, and it will be given you; search, and you will find; knock, and the door will be opened for you. For everyone who asks receives, and everyone who searches finds, and for everyone who knocks, the door will be opened. (7:7–8)

With faith that God will respond to our prayer, it is important to keep our eyes open to the many ways God will work in our lives and the many opportunities for humility that he will send us.

Welcome Opportunities to Grow in Humility

When I first began praying for humility, God immediately gave me many opportunities to grow in this virtue. These opportunities came in the form of small humiliations. Someone would rudely correct me and I would realize that I was being invited to respond peacefully. A person would delightedly point out that I was wrong about something and I would see an invitation to let the comment pass. Eventually, I got fed up with God's pedagogical method and told him so. God helped me to realize that I had been under the false impression that if I prayed for humility, God would promptly infuse me with a humble attitude! Unfortunately, praying for humility is not magic; it does not happen immediately, at least for most people. Instead, slowly, painfully, over time, we learn to accept small humiliations without protest because we know that these opportunities will help us to become more like Jesus.

When we pray for humility, we can sometimes act like a child who wants to learn to swim. God puts us in the water and we immediately scream, "Never mind, the water's cold! This is not fun!" But if we want to grow in humility, we need to both pray for it *and* respond to God's answers to our prayer. God's answers come in the form of little humiliations that either we can forcefully and disdainfully reject, hoping for some other way, or we can accept, trusting that God knows best. If we refuse opportunities to grow in humility yet continue to pray for it, we are ignoring the answer to our prayers and choosing not to respond to the Lord's invitations.

Sometimes interactions with loved ones can be just the opportunity God gives us to become more humble. We may be tempted to get into a heated argument with someone over an aspect of the faith or feel like responding in anger to aggressive anti-Catholicism. In both cases, even if we can eloquently defend our faith, sometimes it is best to refrain from saying anything. It may feel embarrassing to remain silent if we are used to having our say, but a little humiliation is sometimes just what we need to grow in humility. There will be times when our loved ones need to share their feelings without judgment or disagreement on our part, and we may need to learn to listen silently and leave our perfectly reasoned, fabulous arguments unsaid. Or the reverse may be true. We may feel like cowering and running from an argument when God is asking us to humbly and courageously express our faith. In either case, humbly accepting God's will is likely to bear more fruit than eloquent words or fearful silence.

Recognize When Silence Is Best

The virtue of humility enables us to recognize when silence is the best response. It helps us to get in touch with our physical and emotional limits and to recognize when we need to step back. We may be feeling cranky, low on sleep, or just plain irritated. At such moments, we may be unable to respond to a person with humility. If we feel this way and want to lash out at someone on matters of faith, it is best to keep quiet instead. If we lack motivation, we can always remind ourselves that our exercise in self-control is a penance we can offer up for the conversion of our loved ones. This approach will bear much more fruit than harsh words. Even if we do say something inappropriate, it can be a beautiful opportunity to accept the reality that everyone makes mistakes, and then we can make amends. Sometimes humbly asking a person for forgiveness can build trust and improve a relationship. God works through everything.

Respect the Vast Expanse of Truth

In Ephesians 4:15, Paul urges Christians to live "the truth in love" so that we may become more like Christ. When speaking the truth to another person in love, it is important to remember the oft-quoted saying, "Humility is truth." If we keep this in mind, we can communicate the truths of the Church in a Christ-like way. The more Christ-like we are, the more receptive our listeners will likely be to our message.

As members of the Catholic Church, we believe in the truth that Jesus founded the Church. Even when we are confused by something the Church teaches, we can trust that the Holy Spirit guides the Church. If we believe that the faith and moral teachings of the Church can be trusted, despite the failings of human beings who are members of the Church, then this is a grace. In this modern age, to trust a bureaucratic, human institution to guide us in matters of right and wrong is considered naïve or misguided. Amid scandal and sin from within and ridicule and hatred from without, it is a gift from God to continue to have faith in the Church. It does not make sense to take credit for believing something so radically counter-cultural.

However, although we may agree that the Church can be trusted and believed in matters of faith and morals, we have to keep in mind that as human beings we are always traveling in what I like to call "little t" truth territory. In other words, Jesus is the Truth. God is the complete, awe-inspiring Truth. As human beings we have reason, so we can know truth, but we will never fully know Truth (with a big T), at least not in this life. Jesus left us very clear teachings, and the Church continues to teach us with the guidance of the Holy Spirit. We may know these things to be true, but if we are humble, we can be sure that we do not completely understand every aspect of the faith and anything else that we believe to be true.

For example, we can know that a car is green. However, we may not understand how the photoreceptors in our eyes perceive that car to be green. And we also may or may not know that the perception of an object's color is influenced by light and even by the color of the objects nearby. In other words, when we talk truth with those we love, it is always important to keep our limited perspective in mind. We may know what the Church teaches on a certain subject, but it is important to hear objections out. We can approach these objections with humility, not with the idea that the Church may be wrong but that our understanding may be wrong or limited.

When we are open to humbly discussing a person's objections to Church teaching, it is possible to learn a lot, whether we agree with the person's position or not. When we are open to learning from others, they are often much more open to hearing what we have to say. A friend once wisely reminded me of the old adage, "Even a broken watch tells the right time twice a day." It helps to search a person's argument for where he or she might be telling the right time, so to speak. Some people may draw wrong conclusions, but that does not necessarily make everything they say wrong. Even if a person is clearly misled, it is possible and always helpful to assume that he or she will have some salient points and to sincerely search for them in the conversation. Regardless of the situation, an attitude of humility makes sense because it can encourage the foundational attitude that another person needs in order to accept the seed of faith.

Conclusion

> "The younger of [the sons] said to his father, 'Father, give me the share of the property that will belong to me.' So he divided his property between them."

> — Luke 15:12

When the prodigal son demands his inheritance, he in essence is saying, "Father, I wish you were dead." The father does not respond in anger; he simply gives his son what he demands. He does not argue, cajole, or beg; he recognizes that his son is not in a place to hear reason. The father in the parable of the Prodigal Son is the picture of humility. He sees truth and responds to it, without worrying about his personal image or his reputation.

The son, on the other hand, is greatly lacking in humility. He thinks he can live his life apart from the father; he feels he does not need him. So he sets off on his own. This is a very familiar dynamic; we can relate to setting off on our own, whether it lasts for years or just for moments during the day. We have all pushed God away to the point that we feel as if we are in a "distant country," far from the consoling presence of God (see Lk 15:13). This is the dynamic of sin that we all experience.

When the son decides to return home, it is clear that he now sees the truth of the situation: "Father, I have sinned against heaven and before you; I am no longer worthy to be called your son" (Lk 15:21). I am not worthy. These are the words we speak before receiving the Body and Blood of Jesus in the Eucharist. These words are the melody of the song of human relationship with God. Like the prodigal son, we are not worthy of the merciful love of the Father, but we receive it anyway. Why do we receive it? Because the Father, in his humility and love, wants to give us what we do not deserve. But it is only when we see the truth of the situation, when we clearly see our sin, that we are also able to see the Father's mercy.

Humility is the necessary attitude for conversion, for our own and for our loved ones. Let us imitate the Father in his humble love.

CHAPTER THREE

Listening to the Holy Spirit

Christ has no body now on earth but yours,
no hands but yours, no feet but yours;
yours are the eyes through which
Christ's compassion looks out on the world,
yours are the feet with which he is to go about doing good,
and yours are the hands with which
he is to bless us now.

— Attributed to Saint Teresa of Avila

———— ⟡ ————

After my conversion I lived in Oakland, California, for several years. There, I got to know several homeless people who were fixtures in my urban neighborhood. One man, Slim, was lanky, with long, stringy hair that looked like it had not been cut since his hippie days. He wore a wide grin and always seemed delighted to be alive. Billy was another person I saw regularly on the street corners. He sang the blues for passersby and held out his hat for spare change. There were others, but one man stood out from the rest. With matted hair and ragged clothes, he looked like a creature that had just emerged from the forest. He was so dirty that you could see the layers of grime on his skin and black under his fingernails. His face always held a grim, empty expression and his unkempt appearance suggested he was not mentally stable. When he walked down the street, people avoided him by ducking into shops or staring awkwardly at the ground as he passed by.

One day, while driving home from work, I saw this man sitting in the park. As I drove past, I felt an inspiration to buy him something to eat. I knew the idea was probably from the Holy Spirit, but I was scared. So I continued driving home, trying with great difficulty to ignore what I was feeling. I angrily scolded God: "Couldn't you inspire me to help one of the nicer homeless people in the neighborhood?" After driving down the street a few more minutes, I began to feel guilty. "Perhaps the man is really hungry," I thought, "and he is not the type people will try to help; just look at how I am reacting to the idea of buying him some food!" So I made a U-turn and headed to the nearest store. I bought a sandwich, some fruit, and a dessert.

I drove around and spotted the man sitting on a bench, looking exhausted. I parked my car and headed toward him. He caught sight of me walking purposefully his way and leapt off the bench like a startled deer, fear in his eyes. When I arrived at the previously occupied bench, the man was skittishly waiting at an intersection nearby for a walk signal and watching me nervously out of the corner of his eye. I realized that he was as scared of me as I was of him. Since I knew he could see me, I laid the bag of food on the bench and looked at him purposefully. He avoided my gaze.

I left without knowing what would happen next, entrusting the situation to the hands of God. As I walked away, I felt great joy. The feeling was not self-congratulatory joy, but rather the exhilaration of knowing that, because I had listened to God, I had been an instrument of his love.

Inspiration: A Path to Joy

We all have moments when we feel a nudge from the Holy Spirit. But often we want to push it away because, frankly, we desire to control our own lives and are afraid to take risks we have not initiated ourselves. Ever since Adam and Eve took a bite out of that apple, we humans have been trying to do our own thing. We want to follow our own will in the big and the small areas of life. Sometimes we let God in or pray for his guidance, but usually we do this only when we need to make really important decisions or need help. Unfortunately, it is easy to leave God out when it comes to the everyday decisions of our lives.

We often rationalize pushing away the Holy Spirit's inspirations, telling ourselves that we should be able to do what we want, especially when it is not a matter of right or wrong. We may think, "I don't want to call my friend right now; I just want to watch this TV show! What can be wrong with that?" Of course, when the Holy Spirit inspires us, it is never a dictatorial, controlling demand. Even in the case of choosing between right and wrong, God respects that we are human beings whom he created with free will. It is always our free choice to follow the inspirations of the Holy Spirit. But deep down, we know that when we decide to listen to the inspiration of the Spirit, we follow a path of adventure and joy.

To live in union with the Holy Spirit is to live a life of transcendence. Rather than simply existing in our own world with its narrow perspectives and thick walls, we enter the world of free-dom in the Spirit. We push beyond our immediate wants and desires and soon find the exhilarating joy that comes from God acting in and through us. We find the joy of a life lived in the heart of God, and we begin to understand Mother Teresa's words that she is just a pencil in God's hand and that it is God who does the thinking and the writing.

Acting on Inspiration

Following the inspiration of the Holy Spirit is an essential component in our interactions with loved ones who are away from the faith. Unfortunately, there are no blueprints for evangeliza-tion. People do not come with sets of instructions and how-to manuals. This is why it is essential to allow the Holy Spirit to act *within* us. Who knows the hearts of our loved ones better than the Holy Spirit? He knows their wounds, their passions, their desires. He can speak to these things through us, but only if we allow him.

I have a friend who regularly confronts people on issues of faith. She is fearless and very brave. One time, she overheard an acquaintance discussing an immoral behavior he engaged in. My friend told him right away, strongly and forcefully, that what he was doing was wrong. When she told me about it later, I asked her, "Did you feel inspired by the Holy Spirit to say that to him?" She looked at me quizzically; this was not a usual factor in her decision-making.

Now, perhaps my friend did the right thing and what she said had a good effect on the person. However, if she had been inspired to say what she did, she could be more confident that her words would bring the person closer to God. Sometimes it is hard to understand why we need to consult the Holy Spirit before confronting someone, especially if we feel the person is endangering his or her soul. But it is important to understand and respect that people who no longer believe in God or have left the Church are in a delicate spiritual position, often with serious wounds at the source of their feelings about God. Even if the person we are concerned about is a close family member or our own child, we cannot assume we know what a person needs. Only the Holy Spirit knows and fully understands the hearts of our loved ones.

The Holy Spirit has a variety of roles in mind that he may or may not want us to play in a person's life, because he knows exactly what each person needs to grow in faith. He may want us to communicate with someone boldly and frankly because that is the approach needed at that time in their lives. Or, in some cases, he may just want us to show a person gentle, Christian love. If we rely on the Spirit, we can have greater trust that we are acting in a way that is truly beneficial for others. When we act on our own initiative, we have no guarantee that what we do or say will be helpful rather than harmful. With the Holy Spirit, we can be much more confident that we will be effective in our loved ones' lives. We will certainly make mistakes, but it is better to move forward and make a mistake than not to move forward at all.

Identifying True Inspirations

You may think that the idea of acting on the Spirit's inspiration is all well and good, but you have no idea how to go about doing it and may even be unsure whether you have ever heard the Spirit inspire you to do anything. Responding to the Holy Spirit's invitations may seem like a vague concept to you, so ethereal, so beyond everyday life. Hans Urs von Balthasar once described inspirations like so:

Soft it approaches, almost inaudible, and yet quite unavoidable:
a ray of light, an offer of power, a command that is more and less
than a command—a wish, a request, an invitation, an entice-
ment: brief as an instant, simple to grasp as the glance of two
eyes.[1]

How beautiful that sounds, so simple yet at the same time so difficult to grasp, so tricky to detect! And it is true, the inspirations of
the Holy Spirit are not easy to discern and still more difficult to
follow. This may account for the times in our own lives when we
choose to ignore the Holy Spirit's inspirations and stick with what
makes us comfortable. But the truth is that everyone has heard the
voice of the Spirit; most of us just need to get more used to listening and responding to it.

You probably have a friend who calls you on the phone regularly and whose voice has become so familiar that you already
know who it is before he or she tells you. This is how familiar we
want to become with the voice of the Holy Spirit. Father Jacques
Philippe, in his book *In the School of the Holy Spirit*, tells us that in
order to hear the Holy Spirit, we must develop a "spiritual
hearing":

This "spiritual hearing" is a kind of ability to recognize, among
all the multiple, discordant voices that we hear inside us, the
unique, unmistakable voice of Jesus. This sense is like a loving
instinct that makes it easier and easier for us to distinguish the
voice of the Spouse, in the chorus of sounds that greet our ears.[2]

The Holy Spirit speaks to each of us uniquely and so, in order
to live according to his inspirations, we can develop a keen ear for
what his voice sounds like. Silent prayer is how we develop an ear
for the Holy Spirit's unique way of communicating with us; it is
like picking up the phone and regularly talking to a friend whose
voice we begin to recognize and know well. When we give

ourselves quiet time to listen, we tune our ears to the unique melody and timbre of the Holy Spirit's voice in our life. With practice, we can become more confident as we follow his invitations. We develop this sense of what the Spirit's voice sounds like both with prayer *and* by accepting and acting on his inspirations. It doesn't do much good to identify the voice of the Holy Spirit if we still ignore it. Accepting the nudge of the Holy Spirit is like accepting an invitation from a friend to go out for coffee. If we keep saying no, the friend will eventually ask less often.

Discerning the Fruit of Our Actions

We can generally be confident we are acting on the Holy Spirit's initiative and developing our "spiritual sense" correctly if feelings of peace, love, and joy accompany an inspiration. If we act upon inspirations and the fruit of our actions continue to be positive, we can be even more certain that we are hearing the voice of the Holy Spirit. The fruit of our actions often show us whether or not we are walking the path of inspiration.

For example, imagine you just spent an afternoon with a friend who is away from the Church. You asked God throughout your time with this friend to inspire you to mention your faith if it was God's will. At one point in the conversation, you felt an inspiration to share something about your prayer life. You wanted to say much more, but you sensed that it was most likely best to leave it there. After the conversation, you feel peace and joy. Because you asked for God's inspiration, you can confidently surrender to him any comments you made that may not have been helpful or any inspirations you may have missed, knowing that you tried your best and that God appreciates your honest desire to be inspired and led by him.

Of course, we cannot always expect feelings of peace and joy to follow our interactions with loved ones, especially if the Holy Spirit is inspiring us to say something challenging. Our words may actually stir up anger or other negative emotions in the person we love. However, it is important for us to detach to a certain extent from others' reactions and to get in touch with the affirming feelings that the Spirit inspires in us. The peace God provides may be a deep underlying peace. If we have entered into conflict with our loved ones, we may need to really search to find this peace, but it will be there if we are walking in the right path of inspiration. If we find this peace at the foundation of our actions toward another, we can be confident in what we have said or done.

It may be helpful to note that the affirmation of the Holy Spirit is not to be confused with our own self-congratulatory feelings of smugness and self-righteousness when we choose to say something harsh without the Holy Spirit's inspiration. If we unnecessarily cause conflict or hurt another's feelings out of arrogance, fear, or inappropriate anger, it does no good to pretend that we did the right thing. The peace of God should not be confused with misguided self-satisfaction. If we have followed our own bright ideas and said the wrong thing, it is best to admit it to ourselves and to others, and to make amends.

Discerning Unhealthy Motivations

If we feel fear or guilt pushing us to say something to someone we love, it is probably not an inspiration from the Holy Spirit. Often unhealthy feelings and motivations mixed with the urgency they can cause lead us to act or speak in a way that does not bring the person we love closer to God, but instead pushes the person further away. These negative feelings are almost always a sign that we need to take a big breath and pause. Of course, our motivations for what we do will always be a bit mixed, but we can usually identify the primary motivating feeling. If our primary motivation for a planned behavior is fear, frustrated anger, or guilt, then it is usually best to step away from the situation before acting.

A sense of urgency is perhaps one of the most common emotions, and potentially the most damaging, that can negatively impact our interactions with loved ones. If we feel an urgent need to say something to someone as soon as possible, this is usually a sign that we are not in a good place emotionally. Of course, it is beautiful to feel a strong desire to bring someone back to communion with God in the Church. However, when this holy sense of imperative develops an unholy sense of fear and urgency, it will most likely cause us to do and say things that will be ineffective and hurtful. If we feel this sense of urgency, we must ask ourselves, "Where does this come from?" Does our urgency come from trust in the loving providence of God? If not, we should work to leave these feelings behind.

As we are told in the First Letter of John: "There is no fear in love" (1 Jn 4:18). God wants what is best for everyone he loves. There is no reason for us to be fearful or to think that everything depends on us. If we feel fear, it is helpful to explore the source of our fear. Do we want someone to return to the Church because we are scared of what God might do if that person does not return? Certainly hell is a reality, and one that we deeply want our loved ones to avoid. However, true faith is not based in fear. Fear and sorrow for sin play an important part in a person's faith journey, but a faith relationship based in fear will not attract others to the faith; a *love* relationship with God will. When we are in a love relationship with God, we understand deeply just how much he loves us, and we want others to experience this love. Each person is precious and beloved in God's eyes; *this* is why we want them to return to a relationship with him and his Church. When we frame our message in love and hope rather than fear, we place our trust in a God who holds every single person deeply in his heart and wants their salvation even more than we do.

It always makes sense to pause and take time to be sure our actions are founded in and inspired by the love of God. When a sense of urgency guides our behavior, we can easily become confused and caught up in our own heads. Unfortunately this can keep us from looking for the right solutions to the problems we face. When we begin to feel fearful, it is vital to bring our concerns to God in prayer. When we do not pray, especially before important interactions, we may end up saying the wrong thing. Barring some sort of emergency, we always have time to pray before approaching someone. It is also helpful, outside of prayer times, to have our ears open for the various ways the Spirit might speak to us in the events of daily life. The Spirit will ordinarily speak to us through prayer, but he may also speak in a variety of unexpected ways: through a talk, a book we are reading, the advice of a trusted friend, and even a passing comment from a stranger.

Sometimes an emotion generally viewed as negative is actually an appropriate motivation for our actions. This can particularly be true with the emotion of anger. Anger is neither good nor bad; it is simply a feeling that alerts us to something that may need to change. When a loved one crosses our boundaries or the boundaries of others with unacceptable behavior, our anger can alert us to the need to say something. Sometimes our loved ones seriously endanger themselves physically or spiritually, and then our anger can motivate us to say what we need to say. In these times, the Holy Spirit calls on us to act decisively and forcefully. Such moments can particularly occur when parents deal with underage children who seriously need correction. If expressed in a controlled way, the emotion of anger can show we care deeply about those we love.

Sometimes, a person is waiting for a sign that their actions are unacceptable, and our words can be that sign.

However, it is important that our anger be a loving anger. This may sound like an oxymoron, but it is not. Most likely, we can all recall a time when an authority figure was harsh with us simply out of frustration or in an attempt to exert power over us. But we most likely can also remember times when someone expressed anger in a way that made it clear that the person's behavior was motivated by real love. If we are motivated by something other than love, and are not led by the Spirit, expressing anger can be highly damaging to another's spiritual journey. So it is imperative that we act upon the Spirit's inspiration and speak only and always out of love.

No matter what motivates an interaction with loved ones, it can be helpful to observe how the Holy Spirit acts in our own lives to learn how to interact with others. For the most part, the Holy Spirit works slowly and gently within our souls, so it is important to show the same respect to the people we love by approaching slowly and gently, rather than with undue intensity, aggressiveness, or fear.

Learning from Mary

You may be familiar with the passage in the Gospel of Matthew, where Mary and several family members approach Jesus while he is preaching. A disciple tells Jesus that his mother and family are there to speak with him. Jesus looks at his disciples, extends his arm, and says, "Who is my mother?" He goes on to say, "For whoever does the will of my Father in heaven is my brother and sister and mother" (Mt 12:48, 50). At first glance it may sound as if Jesus is disparaging his mother. One imagines Mary overhearing Jesus and thinking, "Well, that is a nice how-do-you-do!" But when Jesus asked, "Who is my mother?" it must have prompted his disciples to think of the mother of Jesus, whom they knew as the humble yet very holy woman whose whole soul was filled with the presence of God.

In asking, "Who is my mother?" Jesus is encouraging us to look to her as a model of holiness. Who indeed is the Mother of Jesus? And what can she teach us about doing the will of the Father? Saint John Paul II once remarked that it is from Mary that we learn how to surrender to God's will in all things.[3] Mary, like her Son Jesus, perfectly united her will to the Father's. She followed the inspirations of the Holy Spirit in all that she did. When an angel appeared to her and told her she would give birth to the Messiah, she humbly received and accepted the message with obedience, joy, and trust. People sing songs, paint pictures, and write poems about the moment of the annunciation, but few of us take the time to let that moment really sink in. Mary's response to the angel Gabriel has been so abundantly analyzed that it is easy to become weary with the repetition and overlook how truly remarkable it is. If we consider her context and situation, it is clear that Mary's ready acceptance of this astounding news is truly incredible. But it was possible because Mary was *already in constant union with the Holy Spirit.* She knew his voice, like we know the voices of our closest friends. When the time came for her to receive the most important inspiration of the Holy Spirit in her life and for the entire history of the world, Mary was ready.

Mary is our model of listening to the gentle voice of the Holy Spirit. Mary understands our needs and concerns. She can help us when we feel lost. She can help us find the courage to speak to our loved ones on the Spirit's inspiration. She can help us pick up the pieces when we say the wrong thing. She can help us if we humbly implore her to intercede for those we love and bring them closer to her Son. Mary is our connection to the Spirit; she can help us learn to know his voice.

Conclusion

"But when he came to himself he said, 'How many of my father's hired hands have bread enough and to spare, but here I am dying of hunger!'"

— Luke 15:17

The moment in which the prodigal son "came to himself" was a moment of inspiration. At the depths of his despair, the son is open to the Holy Spirit working in his heart, helping him to see the situation as it truly is. The disgrace of his poverty does not lie in his lowly job tending swine, although this would have been disgraceful for a Jew; rather the deepest disgrace is the son's disrespect for the father. With the help of the Spirit, the son's sin is clear before his eyes. The Spirit can help us see the interior "spiritual lining" of every situation, to reach below the surface of our lives, and to respond to deeper spiritual realities. This enlightened perspective will help us to acknowledge and respect where our loved ones are and what they can handle. The Holy Spirit then inspires us to behave based on the truth that he helps us to see.

When we act in union with the Spirit's inspirations, we find the courage to act as the Spirit wants, rather than only in ways that we think best. To be "kind" is only meaningful in union with God. To be "loving" is only meaningful in union with God. To be "challenging" or "truthful" is only meaningful in union with God. The Spirit helps us to come to our senses, like the prodigal son, and to see clearly what we need to do and how we need to do it. Let us ask God for the grace to come to our senses as the prodigal son did and to live our lives in truth, according to the inspirations of the Spirit.

CHAPTER FOUR

Finding the Balance: Love and Truth

"There is a widespread belief that one should use the truth even against love or vice versa. But truth and love need each other." [1]

— Saint John Paul II

———◇———

For most of high school, I attended a relatively rural school in Oklahoma where the majority of students were nondenominational Christians, many of whom were very serious about their faith. One day, a girl in my orchestra class asked me whether I accepted Jesus as my Lord and Savior. She was a sweet girl, and we got along well, so I honestly told her that I did not. The conversation quickly unraveled as it became clear that not only did I not accept Jesus, but

I also did not think God existed at all. The girl looked at me in complete shock and disgust, as if I had suddenly become another person. She said several times: "You know that you are in danger of going to hell, don't you!" I had nothing to say to her. Staring at the musical notes in front of me, I thought angrily, "Is this really how you are going to try to convince me to believe in your God?"

Too often when interacting with our loved ones, we simply adopt ways we are comfortable with rather than ways that are actually most helpful. Two common approaches can be found among friends and family of fallen away Catholics. On the one hand, some people say very little. Although they hope their loved one will return to the Church, they never say anything to indicate they are even aware the person no longer attends Mass. On the other hand, however, some people say too much, too often, and too harshly. Their aggressive style of communication can cause rifts in relationships or, at best, lead to tension-filled encounters with those they love.

Kate, a woman who has been away from the Church for many years, describes how faith issues play out in her family:

> My mother wants us to identify as Catholics, definitely. She'd die if she knew I don't "technically" identify. But to diss Catholicism in front of her would be like dissing my beloved ninety-two-year-old grandma. I just wouldn't do it. It's sacred, like a treasured family member.

Many families like Kate's avoid discussing faith, sometimes to evade conflict or to escape heartbreak. Other families discuss faith issues in ways that are controlling, aggressive, and manipulative. Neither of these approaches is helpful. Our friends and family members are not likely to come back to the Church if we never express our desire for them to return, but if we express our desire in a way that turns them off, chances are they will not return either.

You may identify with one of these extreme ways of approaching faith issues with your loved ones or you may find yourself wavering between them, desperately trying to find the right balance. In order to love, we must love truthfully. Those who lean more toward gentleness, and say too little, may be lacking in their ability to love *truthfully*, while those who tend to be too aggressive may be lacking in *charity*. When we express love without truth, our love becomes an empty shell that does not express anything substantial or meaningful. When we express truth without love, it is like trying to hang a picture without a nail. We can hammer away in truth, but if we do not say it in love, our words will most likely hurt others and be ineffective. God ultimately invites us to communicate both love *and* truth in our lives, in the deepest sense of both words, and he calls us to a beautiful balance of both.

Jesus is the ideal and model for how we can love others in truth. As Pope Benedict XVI writes in the encyclical *Charity in Truth (Caritas in Veritate)*: "In Christ, charity in truth becomes the Face of his Person, a vocation for us to love our brothers and sisters in the truth of his plan."[2] In other words, when we love in truth, we love like Jesus. And when we love like Jesus, we invite the people we love to follow God's plan for their lives. This is the most effective way to bring those we love back to the Church. Several aspects of Jesus's behavior can concretely help us to approach others in a Christ-like way and gently invite them back into relationship with God.

Create a "Table of Acceptance"

As you may know, tax collectors in the time of Jesus were social pariahs. They were in collaboration with Gentile Roman occupiers and were known to exact more than was required. Their very work was considered sinful, making tax collectors immoral and unclean in the eyes of the people. For this reason, they were often ostracized from the Jewish community. Yet, Jesus ate at the home the tax collector Matthew. And Scripture tells us that "many tax collectors and sinners came and were sitting with him and his disciples" (Mt 9:10). Note that Jesus did not go and sit with sinners, but they "came and sat" with him. That they would dare to sit at the table of a virtuous Jew demonstrates the radical acceptance that Jesus must have shown them. They could sense that Jesus accepted and affirmed who they were and who they could be, unlike the self-righteous people who disdained them and avoided their company.

What did these sinners experience at the Lord's table? It is unlikely that Jesus spent mealtimes focusing on his companions' sins. Rather, sinners most likely wanted to be in his company because they recognized someone who loved them. Jesus did not judge them, yet at the same time he effectively urged people to change their behavior through genuine love and respect for their human dignity. It may be helpful to ask ourselves what others experience at our "tables" of conversation and everyday interactions. Does our behavior inspire a sense trust in others? Do people feel comfortable approaching us with their concerns and fears without feeling like they will be judged? Do we spread our table with radical acceptance, love, and respect?

Jesus felt it was important to emphasize the dignity and value of people who were often rejected by others. Do we act like Jesus when we relate to people who are away from the Church, or do we behave like the self-righteous who are more concerned with their own purity than with reaching out? Often we associate truth with what is uncomfortable or causes others to feel shame. Rather, if we are the kind of people who appreciate truth, perhaps Jesus is calling us to focus on the truth that those we love are beautiful, precious, and beloved in the eyes of God, no matter their sin. We can begin to recognize this when we accept that this is the truth of our own relationship with God. Saint Paul writes in the Letter to the Romans that "God proves his love for us in that while we still were sinners Christ died for us" (5:8). We do not deserve God's love, yet he loves and accepts us. We are called to love others in this same way.

Love First, Without Limits

God's love has no limits or conditions. The First Letter of John tells us that "we love because he first loved us" (1 Jn 4:19). In other words, God's love precedes our love. We do not have to love God in order for him to love us. He loves us before we even have the chance to reject his love. He loves and then invites us to experience his love. For a person away from the Church, God's unconditional love is a very important reality to understand. By modeling this love, we can help others to understand the nature of God. God doesn't love us on the condition that we love him or that we stop sinning. His love has no contingencies, qualifications, or contracts. God loves us now, as we are. We do not have to change before God loves us, and it is precisely this kind of love that *does* change us.

The story of Zacchaeus (Lk 19:1–10) demonstrates the nature of God's unconditional love. Before Zacchaeus even met Jesus, he "was trying to see who Jesus was" (19:3). His curiosity prompted him to disregard social propriety and, like a carefree child, to climb a sycamore tree. Saint John Paul II described Zacchaeus's curiosity as the fruit of the mercy of God which preceded Zacchaeus and drew him to Jesus. The desire to know Jesus is part of the dynamic of God's love; it is a grace that prepared the heart of Zacchaeus for conversion and change, and it is a grace that God can make available to all of our loved ones.

The grace that prepared the heart of Zacchaeus for conversion came from the very overflow of love that God had for him and for each one of us. Zacchaeus does not waste this grace of desire but rather searches Jesus out and is rewarded. Jesus stops in front of Zacchaeus and asks the infamous town tax collector if he can stay at his house. Of all the people in town, Jesus knowingly chooses to stay at the house of a public sinner. In fact, he not only chooses to stay with Zacchaeus, Jesus seems to urgently desire to spend time with him. He says, "I *must* stay at your house" (19:5, emphasis added). Jesus is not afraid to show Zacchaeus his great desire to be in his company. The words and actions of Jesus show that God's love for us is urgent and palpable.

Jesus takes a risk by offering an invitation of friendship to Zacchaeus, leaving him free to accept or not. God loves us so much that he pours out his mercy and love on us *before* we respond. He does not wait to see if we will waste his graces; rather he gives them to us knowing we will have the freedom to reject them or not. Jesus shows this kind of love in his extravagant display of acceptance and affection toward Zacchaeus. This risk, the excess of love that Jesus shows Zacchaeus, initiates a conversion in his heart. Zacchaeus could reject Jesus, but instead he is moved to give up his bad behavior. He says, "Look, half of my possessions, Lord, I will give to the poor; and if I have defrauded anyone of anything, I will pay back four times as much" (19:8).

Risking rejection by showing an abundance of love is something that moves hearts. The story of Zacchaeus teaches us this special quality of God's love that we are invited to model. We are called to pour out our love on others, including (and especially) those who are far from God. We are called to do this even at the risk of our love being wasted or rejected. We take the risk because when others see God's loving invitation expressed through us, it may call them to examine their relationship with their Creator and desire to make some changes in their lives. While it is never risky to be judgmental, it is almost always risky to be merciful. Jesus takes risks in love, and he invites us to do the same. Certainly this is difficult to do, but as the conversion of Zacchaeus demonstrates, when it succeeds it really succeeds.

Establish Trust, Attract, Then Challenge

Jesus approaches sinners with gentle love and acceptance, often without saying anything directly about their sins—and hearts are converted. Jesus reserves harshness for those who are self-righteous. He tries to shake the self-righteous out of their complacency so they will recognize their hardness of heart and blindness to their own sin. Jesus does not mince words, calling such people "blind fools," "hypocrites," and "whitewashed tombs" (Mt 23:17, 23, 27). But Jesus approaches those on the margins of Jewish society, those who have rejected the law, in a radically different way. He proceeds by showing care and respect, laying a foundation of love and trust before challenging their behavior.

Take the passage of the Samaritan woman in the Gospel of John (4:1–42). When Jesus meets her at the well, he does not immediately challenge her sinful lifestyle. That is not the first thing on his mind. Rather, Jesus asks the woman for a drink, knowing that receiving water from a Samaritan woman would make him ritually unclean. Like sitting at table with sinners, Jesus breaks ritual law to show the woman that he does not reject her; he is not concerned about avoiding her because she is unclean. With this gesture of acceptance, Jesus initiates a conversation based on mutual trust.

After Jesus gains the woman's trust, he speaks to her of the living water that he is able to give her. Jesus tells her that "those who drink of the water that I will give them will never be thirsty. The water that I will give will become in them a spring of water gushing up to eternal life" (4:14). Before Jesus confronts the woman's sinful behavior, he gives her a glimpse of why she would want to change. Living in the path of God gives us access to living water. Someone must see the attraction, joy, and exhilaration in such a life in order to desire to change. We can be models of this joy, this living water, which is the Christian life.

When Jesus sees that the woman truly desires this living water and she asks for it, only then does he tell her that he knows she has had five husbands. Jesus says, "You are right in saying, 'I have no husband'; for you have had five husbands, and the one you have now is not your husband. What you have said is true!" (4:18). He does not tell her this to condemn her but to indicate that he is aware of her behavior and he desires conversion in her heart. I imagine that as he said these words Jesus looked at the woman with gentle frankness, but also with deep love and a desire to be closer to her.

It is the way Jesus approaches the woman that helps him to win her heart. His priorities are first to establish a foundation of trust, to show the woman the beauty of living a life with God, and *then* to challenge her simply, gently, and succinctly. Jesus does not dwell on the Samaritan woman's sin. He simply invites her to leave her old life behind, a life of trying to quench a thirst unquenchable by sin, so that she may satisfy her thirst in God.

The woman's actions following the conversation reveal that Jesus's words inspired her rather than made her feel unduly ashamed or paralyzed. The woman is so excited that she leaves her water jar as she runs to town (4:28). This symbolic action, carefully recorded in Scripture, helps us to understand the earth-shattering change that Jesus has initiated in this woman's life. She has chosen to respond affirmatively, in complete freedom, to the invitation to leave her old life behind. She leaves her water jar, that which provides physical water to sustain her, for God, the source of living water. The woman's action echoes Peter and Andrew's response to Jesus: "Immediately they left their nets and followed him" (Mt 4:20). Like Peter and Andrew, this woman has left her old life behind to become a disciple of Jesus.

The story of the Samaritan woman is a powerful one to contemplate before challenging your loved one's behavior. When we challenge someone we love, no matter what we say, our words are likely to sound like an attack unless we have established a foundation of love and trust with the person. If our loved ones are convinced that we love and respect them, our words will take on a softer tone in their minds and they will be more likely to respond as the Samaritan woman responded to Jesus. We can either frame our challenges in charity, gentle honesty, and acceptance, or in disappointment and rejection. It is up to us to maximize the potential power our words can have in the lives of those we love.

It may help to contemplate how the icon of the woman at the well is present in our own spiritual lives. God often prepares our hearts by establishing trust and showing us love before he challenges us. When we are sure of our role as beloved children of God, then we can accept challenges as something that will bring us closer to God. God knows how to convert our hearts. We can imitate this pattern of God's love in our relationships by first focusing on accepting others and establishing trust with them. In the end, we can only really act in truth and love if we imitate Truth and Love. If we get to know Jesus more through prayer, reading Scripture, and receiving the sacraments, we will continually become more and more Christ-like. By following and observing Jesus, we can be more effective in gently urging our loved ones closer to the One who loves them deeply and profoundly. Learning to love in truth is learning to let Jesus love in truth *within* us. We can only love like Jesus if he does it for us. So we ask him to live within us, act within us, and love within us, so that we may love others in a way that draws them nearer to Christ.

The beautiful interplay of truth and love in our lives is an adventure. God asks us to learn how to communicate and love in *his* way, not ours. On our part it will require change, flexibility, and a deep humility. But we can learn. Jesus laid the groundwork. He converted peoples' hearts effectively with the perfect balance of truth and love. Not everyone responded positively to the invitations of Jesus. Not everyone will respond positively to our invitations. But the more we love in truth like Jesus, the more successfully we will draw others to the Church.

Conclusion

> "This son of mine was dead and is alive again; he was lost and is found!"
>
> — Luke 15:24

The father does not mince words; his son was dead. The prodigal son had been spiritually lifeless, cut off from the vine of life. But now, the son has returned and is alive. The father cannot hide his joy, love, and excitement. It is not the "dead" that matters now, but the "alive." We learn from the father that truthful love looks at the positive, at the growing edge of our loved ones' behavior. Love is not naïve, but it is hopeful. Love sees not only what is but what can be. Love hopes, even in the face of circumstances that do not look entirely hopeful.

It is possible that the prodigal son's repentance was not sincere. It is possible that he ran away from his father the day after his return. The father does not base his profuse display of love on guarantees that his son will not sin again. His love is generous and boundless, regardless of the son's response. But the father also loves him in truth. He does not pretend that his son has done nothing wrong. He does not welcome him without a word about his behavior. No, the father admits the son was dead. The behavior of the son was so destructive that he considered him dead, not because the father wanted him to be dead, but because the son chose to be. But the father does not dwell on the past. The higher truth of our existence is not the truth of our sin but that we are redeemed sinners. We are truly who we are meant to be *in Christ*. Our mistakes are not our true identity.

Truth, therefore, is that God's mercy and love overflow to cover our sins. God's grace overwhelms our sins. This is why the father does not even wait to hear the son's apology. God's grace even precedes our repentance. The Father's grace meets us, like the father in the parable met his son on the road, while we are "still far off," far before we reach perfect repentance. This is how truth meets love, and how we are called to meet our loved ones. Let us then be like a father who leaves behind all decorum and excitedly runs down the road to breathe life into his son with acceptance and unremitting mercy.

CHAPTER FIVE

Responding to Illusory Ideas

"Fallacies . . . do not cease to be fallacies because they become fashions."[1]

— G. K. Chesterton

<hr />

Once on a plane ride to California I sat next to a young Latino man who was raised Catholic but had left the faith to become a Buddhist. We had a friendly conversation about our religious backgrounds and spiritual beliefs. We agreed on many things and the conversation was warm. At one point he said to me, "I really think that in the end all religions help humans to become better humans. Buddha and Jesus, for instance, were both exemplary human beings." I agreed, but then said with great passion,

"But Jesus was not only human—he was also God, unique and singular, not god-like but God. That is the essential difference between Buddha and Jesus." The young man smiled at me, surprised at my sudden excitement. He seemed disappointed that we had reached a point of disagreement, but I actually felt some relief. Although there was a lot of common ground between our religions, the conversation would not have been as honest and real had we not reached this key point of disagreement.

The young man I met on the plane expressed a sentiment common among people today—that all religions are equally valid. This is just one of many ideas we might face when interacting with loved ones. It is important to be aware of the various ways our loved ones can be influenced so that we can respond thoughtfully and with patience. It helps to keep in mind that we are also negatively affected by the erroneous ideas in our society. All of us are immersed in a social and cultural context of ideas that seem reasonable and benign, but ultimately can undermine and endanger the health of our faith. Many things influence us, consciously and unconsciously, that can, in the end, harm our relationship with God.

Some ways of thinking and approaching life—so common we hardly notice them—act like subtle toxins that can cloud the waters of faith life for us and others. We examine some of these ideas not to judge or pretend that we are superior to our loved ones, but in order to relate and respond to them better. This chapter will only briefly cover some negative influences common today, but it is hoped that these reflections will help you to consider the unique situations of your loved ones, identify the attitudes that may be leading them away from God, and respond in an appropriate, understanding manner.

The Winds of Relativism

Cardinal Joseph Ratzinger, who later became Pope Benedict XVI, once defined one of the most problematic ways of thinking in today's world: "Relativism, that is letting oneself be 'tossed here and there, carried about by every wind of doctrine' seems the only attitude that can cope with modern times."[2]

Relativism can express itself in either the denial of objective truth, or the denial that objective truth can be discovered or known. Many individuals in our society believe they can choose their own "morally neutral" philosophies of life, leaving God in the dust, as well as hope for a common, discoverable truth. When this happens, truth often ends up determined in the court of majority opinion. This is a frightening prospect, especially in the United States because our democracy relies on mutually recognized truths in order to exist. The fact that these attitudes have crept into our culture is a sign of estrangement from God. If we do not believe or trust in God, how can we rely on him to reveal truth to us? Relativism denies the existence of a God who is powerful and can reveal himself as Truth in human history.

Relativistic ideas are behind the legalization of abortion (what is wrong for you is okay for me) and these attitudes continue to endanger human life and religious freedom around the world. Simply put, the influence of relativism in our society is dangerous. However, it is important to keep in mind that people who adopt these harmful views are often well-meaning, intelligent, and compassionate people. Relativists easily see situations from many vantage points. They know we live in a complex world and do not pretend to completely understand it. Relativists are often turned off by arrogant claims to truth; they are sensitive to others' needs and have compassion for people who find themselves in difficult situations. Because relativists often have some key things right, it is difficult to argue against their ideas without coming across as close-minded and dogmatic.

One issue that helps to keep in mind is the concept of extenuating circumstances. Relativists often believe that subjective circumstances should be taken into consideration when considering the morality of an act. In a sense, relativists are on to something here. When a person acts in an immoral way, circumstances such as psychological makeup, family and cultural background, and many other things can influence and partially excuse a person's behavior. Relativists are right to say that these subjective circumstances are important to keep in mind when considering a person's actions. But relativists get it wrong when they argue that these circumstances make it impossible to determine whether or not an action is moral. Morality is determined not only by circumstances and an individual's subjective intention, but also by the nature of an act itself.

When a person is judged by God, subjective circumstances may indeed lessen the severity of an individual's guilt in God's eyes. God is a just judge. A person who steals because he is poor is probably at a different level of sin than a person who simply steals for the thrill of it. We can trust that God, in his mercy, considers the disposition of a person's heart in judging his or her behavior. Unfortunately, the relativist often takes one step beyond recognizing this truth and excuses the person's behavior completely. By doing this, the relativist assumes the role of God. God is the only one who can wipe away our sins. And in wiping away our sins, God does not even go as far as the relativist; he does not pretend that the sins he wipes away were never sins in the first place.

However, it is important to understand that the relativist is right in insisting that we should not judge. We have all heard the saying, "hate the sin, love the sinner." That saying originates from a phrase in one of Saint Augustine's letters: *Cum dilectione hominum et odio vitiorum*, which translates roughly: "With due love for the persons and hatred of the sin."[3] This idea is repeated ad nauseam by Christians, but too often we do not act in a way that is truly consistent with the spirit behind it. We must fight the human tendency to judge those in sin, to show disgust or act like we are superior. We must try to spare our loved ones this bad example. Even if we betray our judgment in something as simple as a strained tone of voice, it is better to keep silent. A judgmental attitude understandably sets off alarms in the hearts of our loved ones, not to mention it is the opposite of the Christ-like behavior we are called to model. Judgmental behavior can push others further from the oasis of faith into the desert of relativism.

Another key issue that often comes up with relativists concerns various forms of the idea the young man on the plane expressed—that all religions are equal paths to the same goal. Depending on the precise ideas and assumptions behind this sentiment, the relativist may again be on to something, and it is important to be balanced in our response to this point of view. The first key point to keep in mind is that as Catholics, we believe that non-Catholics and non-Christians *can* be accepted into heaven. But at the same time, the grace for salvation is only found securely through Christ and in the Church.

In his encyclical *Mission of the Redeemer* (*Redemptoris Missio*), Saint John Paul II wrote: "It is necessary to keep these two truths together, namely, the real possibility of salvation in Christ for all mankind and the necessity of the Church for salvation."[4] Due to the unsurpassed generosity and limitlessness of God's mercy, the boundaries of the Church, through which we are saved, are indeterminable from a human perspective. If we pretend to know whether people of other religions will make it to heaven, we neither express our Catholic faith nor do we provide a good example to our loved ones. On the other hand, if we shrug our shoulders and pretend it makes no difference whether someone is Christian, we do no justice to the truth that Jesus, in his fullness, is not found in other religions. Our religion holds a treasure—and within the Church the *complete* treasure—which all other religions are seeking.

This is not to say that we are better than people who belong to other religions. Embarrassingly, there are non-Christians who are more Christ-like in their actions than many Christians. How is this possible? Because people can grow close to God through other religions. The Vatican II document *On the Relation of the Church to Non-Christian Religions* (*Nostra Aetate*), states:

> The Catholic Church rejects nothing that is true and holy in [other] religions. She regards with sincere reverence those ways of conduct and of life, those precepts and teachings which, though differing in many aspects from the ones she holds and sets forth, nonetheless often reflect a ray of that Truth which enlightens all men.[5]

We believe Christ is the light of the world (see Jn 8:12). He shines for the *entire* world to see. Many religions are open to this light, and without knowing Jesus explicitly they are like mirrors reflecting the light of Christ to others. We can find rays of truth, rays of Christ, in other religions. That being said, any religion that does not know Christ explicitly will not have the fullness of light. Jesus *is*, as we state in the Creed, "God from God, Light from Light." Jesus is the Truth that all religions seek, and he resides in the Body of Christ, the Church. If we do not know the person of Jesus, then we cannot fully know God.

In discussing other religions with someone who feels it is arrogant to claim that our faith holds the truth, we can both affirm the truth found in other religions *and* affirm that the entirety of truth is found in Jesus, who resides in the Church. If we lose the balance between both of these truths, we risk pushing the sensitive hearts of our loved ones even further away. We should not fear that affirming the truth found in other religions will lead our loved ones away from the Church. At the same time, we must take care not to affirm other religions without pointing out that a religion that lacks Jesus is like an apple pie without apples. A pie without apples may still be sweet, like a religion without Jesus may still contain the sweetness of God. But any religion that does not explicitly recognize Jesus is missing a key ingredient. He is the truth that all other religions are seeking.

This discussion also applies to loved ones who still believe in Jesus and may belong to another Christian faith but are away from the Catholic Church. It is important to affirm the common ground between us, which is Jesus. But at the same time we cannot shrug and pretend that it makes no difference if a loved one comes back to the Church or not. The fullness of grace in the sacraments, and therefore the fullness of Jesus, is within the Church. Our Christian brothers and sisters understand the gift of Baptism that makes us all adopted sons and daughters of God. However, it is within the Church that this gift of the indwelling of the Trinity within us can be nurtured and our union with God increased through the graces and the healing power of the sacraments.[6]

A particularly important sacrament for our growth in union with God is found in the true Presence of Jesus in the Eucharist. According to the *Dogmatic Constitution on the Church* (*Lumen Gentium*), a document of Vatican II, the Eucharist is the "source and summit" of our faith.[7] The Catholic Church possesses many more treasures that help a person grow closer to Jesus, but the Eucharist is the most essential, insofar as it is Jesus himself. When we receive the Eucharist, we receive God into our souls, not in a vague symbolic way, but in a real substantial way—it is the Body and Blood of Jesus. If we truly believe this, then we will desperately want to share it with our loved ones who accept Jesus but not his Church. If we are not convinced of the Real Presence of Jesus in the Eucharist, then it may be helpful to learn more about this treasure and spend more time with Jesus before the Blessed Sacrament. Jesus truly lives in the tabernacles of parishes everywhere.

Spiritual Individualism

Linked to the currents of relativism in our society is the growing trend of extreme individualism in all forms. Pope Francis describes our world as being "wounded by a widespread individualism which divides human beings, setting them against one another as they pursue their own well-being."[8]

Religious individualism, the type most relevant to this discussion, is evident in the growing numbers of young people who no longer associate themselves with any particular Christian denomination. Today, many young people gladly accept the label "spiritual" and even "Christian" but at the same time they reject organized religion. Your loved ones may consider themselves to be "spiritual," but no longer go to church. Or they may be churchgoing Christians who have left the Catholic Church. When a person splinters away from the unity found in the Church, it can be a result of excessive individualism.

To be clear, individualism is not always at the root of why Catholics join other Christian faiths. Sometimes Catholics fall away from a faith they did not know well, and into a relationship with Jesus. Kelly, who was baptized Catholic but is now a nondenominational Christian, explains how she felt about her time as a Catholic after she left the Church:

I was angry that while I had heard the words, they were memorized recitations, not personal, and no one had gone deeper to explain that to me. I was mad that I had been so close for so long and no one helped me understand.

This personal relationship with Jesus is something that many fallen-away Catholics find in other Christian faiths. And thank God they do. We must begin with this attitude. God is so good that he meets people where he is able to meet them. If, in our Catholic parishes, someone is not taught how to meet Jesus in a personal way, or is not open to it at the time, then we must be grateful to our other Christian brothers and sisters for introducing our loved ones to Jesus. Knowing Jesus is the first and most important step in faith. If your loved ones have made this step with the help of other Christians, we can only be grateful and give sincere thanks to God.

However, we cannot stop at gratitude, if only because we are aware of the *fullness* of grace that God provides his children within the Church. Aware of this reality, and desiring to share this treasure with those we love, we continue to allow the Holy Spirit to guide interactions with our loved ones, and, when the time is right, to invite them to consider returning to the Church. We cannot grow complacent because, no matter how we look at it, every person's soul thirsts for the sacramental life of the Church. Knowing the importance of the sacraments on an experiential level, and striving to understand them more on an intellectual level is one of the best ways we can combat religious individualism, both in ourselves and in others. When we are attached securely to the presence of Jesus in the Church, we have a firm foundation from which to speak with others who are away.

Religious individualism also fosters the idea that it is not necessary to participate in a church community. It is easy to fall into the trap of thinking that one can "go it alone" and find God without community. Or if a person does choose to participate in a community, it may only be a comfortable one, made up exclusively of like-minded people. This independent, choice-oriented, and self-sufficient way of approaching life is common in the Western world. It is easy to slip into thinking it is possible to live an isolated spiritual life without relying on others and the diversity of the Church that calls us to transformation.

So, what relevance does this have for our loved ones? When people fall away from organized religion and believe they can be "spiritual" either alone or in a small group of people, they will likely begin to create their own realities and truths, not based on the Gospel, but on their own self-determined values. We can help others move away from self-isolating individualism by recognizing it first in our own lives and asking God to help us accept others, even when we disagree and our differences are great. We also can escape individualism by working to come out of ourselves and serve our friends and family, those in our Church community and those in the broader society who need help. Despite the difficulties we are bound to encounter, if we persist we will be an example to others of how real community, with all its pain and joy, helps us as naturally relational beings to grow in holiness. We cannot become holy alone.

Struggles with Church Teaching .

Individualism can also surface in the way many people, including Catholics, view the Church. Pope Francis describes the Church as a mother who "speaks to her child, knowing that the child trusts that what she is teaching is for his or her benefit, for children know that they are loved."[9] Unfortunately, many people approach Church teaching with distrust because our society tells us that as intelligent, rational people, we have a responsibility to weigh what the Church teaches and throw out anything that does not make sense to us. This individualistic way of approaching religion uproots faith, because faith, in its essence, while soaring *on* the wings of reason, also flies *beyond* reason. As the classical formula *supra rationem, non contra rationem* states, faith is *above* reason, but not against it.

Unfortunately, many people claim to disagree with Church teaching on the basis of reason. However, their concept of reason is highly individualistic and relativistic. They limit their assent only to those things that they personally can understand and bring themselves to agree with. Unfortunately, when we rely solely on our own abilities to understand, we cannot have faith because faith is so much more than what we can understand! Faith is a gift from God. And without the firm foundation of faith we cannot hope to fly beyond our limited human ability to reason. So, rather than be open to where faith might be able to illumine our human reasoning, many people prefer to set up their own personal magisterium, judging for themselves what is true and what is not true.

However, when we separate our faith from our reason, we *damage* our ability to reason. God, through the virtue of faith, sheds light on our reason. If a person rejects the faith, he separates the source of faith, God himself, from his ability to reason. Reason without God may appear logical, but it is not as likely to be true. Our reason helps us to reach toward faith, to understand the faith, but ultimately our faith is not something our reason will fully grasp because faith is rooted in God, and God is beyond our reason. This is why our approach to the teaching of the Church, although helped by our reason, must be grounded in faith. So, when we disagree with teachings of the Church, we must ask ourselves, "Do I believe God is guiding the Church, which hands this teaching down to me?"

If God is guiding the Church, then we can submit our reason to this faith. When we submit to the faith, even if we do not understand, God sheds light on our reason and helps us to understand. Unfortunately, many people who disagree with Church teaching do not choose to humbly submit their reason to their faith, and therefore are unable to experience the light of God shining upon the darkness of their reasoning. If we truly believe God guides the Church, then there are only a few possible scenarios for us when we disagree with Church teaching. The first is to accept that we most likely do not fully understand the issue and we need the light of God to shine on our reason. In some cases (for example, where Church teaching has not been fully defined) we can hope that what we disagree with will change. Or we may hope and pray that the way a certain doctrine is articulated by the Church will develop under the patient guidance of the Holy Spirit. Either way, it is most prudent to humbly suspend judgment and trust in God.

For some of us it may be easy to accept the teachings of the Church, while for others it might be much more difficult. This can be due to many things. For one, God has mercifully made us all with different temperaments, abilities, and skills. Combine that with life experiences that have shaped our worldviews, and you get many reasons for people feeling the way they do, some good, some bad, and some neutral. What is important is not whether or not we struggle with Church teaching but rather *how* we do, or do not, struggle.

Whether we accept Church teaching easily or have worked hard to do so, it is important to have sympathy and understanding for those who struggle. We should try to put ourselves in another's shoes and imagine what it is like for them. Also, if we struggled at one point with Church teaching but now do not, we should not assume someone else struggles in the same way or for the same reasons. From speaking to many people who disagree with Church teaching, I have found that most, rather than being arrogant, are feeling great pain and confusion. It is so important, when we interact with others on these topics, to be able to sympathize and understand where they are coming from, even if we do not agree. If a person struggling with Church teaching finds us arrogant, this will not help them to change their mind.

If we ourselves struggle with Church teachings, the important thing is that we do so humbly and with faith so that we can be a *model* for our loved ones. If accepting Church teaching is difficult for us, then our example of humble waiting and trusting in the Lord is a sign to others that belonging to the Church does not mean that we have to understand everything, or even accept it on a human level. God is beyond our human struggles with Church teaching; he is much more powerful, intelligent, and wise than we are. Modeling our belief in God's, and hence the Church's, trustworthiness can be a confounding sign of communion in a world that has elevated individualistic attitudes above all else.

The Noise of the World

God made us with hungers deep enough to be satisfied only by him. This was a dangerous move on his part. He knew that due to original sin we would not always try to satisfy these profound hungers in the right way. Unfortunately, we are often caught up in trying to satisfy our cravings with power, money, material goods, and many other things that God knows will never satisfy the unquenchable longing of our hearts. Only God's infinity is made to fill the gnawing yearning we sometimes feel rumbling beneath our daily activities. That is why no matter how much we acquire, we never feel we have enough. Just when we think we are satisfied,

we are plunged into a feeling of meaninglessness, wondering if anything or anyone is ever going to give us what we need. This need
that we feel so profoundly is God.

The good news is that our loved ones have these hungers as
well. We can be confident that nothing, except a relationship with
God, will ever come close to satisfying them. The bad news is that
our culture is radically oriented to silencing the grumbling of our
spiritual stomachs. Just when we feel like crying out for help, our
mouths are stuffed with food, our outstretched arms are filled with
shopping bags, and our ears, straining to listen, are plugged with
headphones.

Of course, we struggle with this reality too. You might be
wondering what you can do to help your loved one to listen to
God when you find it extremely difficult yourself. The first thing
we can do is model the value of silence. We do this when we
attend Mass, when we incorporate silence into our recreation,
and when we set aside time in our day to recollect ourselves.
Because of the lack of silence in our lives, when we spend time
with our loved ones it can be helpful to do something that brings
the level of activity *down* for them, not up. For example, going
for a hike or a walk together, looking at art, or going camping are
all calming activities that allow for silence. They are also neutral;
they allow our loved ones to connect with God without their
even knowing it.

Of course, if your loved one is open to it, going to Eucharistic
adoration for a short while is also an excellent activity. It is not as
much of a commitment as a Mass, and it is completely silent so
those we love do not have to analyze or intellectualize anything.
Most importantly, they are right there in the Real Presence of
Jesus. You might be surprised by how many self-proclaimed atheists or agnostics are open to this; they are curious and their hearts

often long for contemplation. The Holy Spirit is powerfully active, especially if we pray or make sacrifices before inviting our loved ones to adoration. Don't underestimate God's grace!

Stay Positive

Pope Francis describes the danger of negativity as "one of the more serious temptations which stifles boldness and zeal" and "turns us into querulous and disillusioned pessimists, 'sourpusses.'"[10] Of course, when we think about all the darkness in the world that can lead our loved ones astray, it is easy to become paranoid, to compartmentalize, and to be negative. None of these things, however, is the least bit helpful. Too often, people of faith spend far too much time grousing and grumbling about a world going down the tubes. But what exactly about a sinister and gloomy worldview do we think will attract someone outside the Church?

We are sons and daughters of a God who has overcome the world. If we believe this in love and trust, we can embrace our loved ones with joy, even when their attitudes and beliefs concern us. With the help of Church teaching and the Spirit, we can respond to our loved ones' viewpoints objectively and in a discerning way, sifting the good from the bad. When we focus on the divine in the world rather than evil, it becomes easier to identify what is good and true in our loved ones' ideas, rather than dwell on the bad. It always helps to add some refining comments and point out where we think our loved ones may be missing something, but ultimately we are not trying to get others to think like us, we are trying to bring them closer to the greatest good: God. And if we gradually grow in our own ability to see God in the world, then we will be more effective in helping our loved ones to see him too.

Conclusion

"There he squandered his property in dissolute living."

— Luke 15:13

The prodigal son breaks with tradition when he demands his father's property before his father passes away. Then, to compound the dishonor, the son squanders the property in "dissolute" living. *Asotos* is the Greek word for "dissolute" and it is the negative of *sozo*, the Greek word for "save." In other words, the prodigal son does not save his father's property and care for it, but instead he does the opposite. He wastes what his father gave him.

As the prodigal son threw away his inheritance, so we throw away the inspired intellectual tradition of the Church when we buy in to prevailing ideas of the times that conflict with the teachings of the Church. We all do this. We do it when we are wasteful of the resources that God has given us. We do it when we spend money as if it belonged to us and not to God. We do it when we reject the teachings of the Church with little thought and without even the courtesy of studying and trying to understand the development of Church teaching over the past 2,000 years. We do it when we forget the poor and live our spiritual lives as if they did not exist. We are all the prodigal son, throwing away the riches of our Father for the false ideas of the world.

So we pray that we will recognize the hunger that we are left with when we reject truth and accept a false substitute. We pray that our loved ones will recognize that they also need the richness of our Father's wisdom. May God help us to see that we are like the prodigal son in the time of famine; we always need our Father. God wants to give us the richness of his wisdom through the faith and in prayer. With God's aid, let us reject illusory ideas that do not satisfy and help our loved ones find sustenance in God.

CHAPTER SIX

Accepting Doubt and Embracing Doubters

"Faith can overcome unbelief only by embracing it." [1]

— Father Tomáš Halík

❖

The first year I taught third grade in Teach for America, I had one mischievous student whom I will never forget. Abraham was very bright, with a smile that could light up an entire room, and a frown that was equally dark. When he was bored or frustrated, he found creative ways to express his feelings. Sometimes he would sing and play drumbeats on his desk or delicately balance a book on his head and moo like a cow. As a stressed-out new teacher, Abraham's antics drove me absolutely crazy, but deep down I had a special love for the little troublemaker. I could see my own rebellious nature in his curiosity, constant challenges, and inevitable dissent. I loved him because I knew that his comfort with nonconformity, if nurtured in the right way, could become something beautiful.

In the classroom of life, I believe that God has a similar love for nonconformists, doubters, and seekers. God knows, better than we do, that the very questions that push people away will often bring them back, to reside in a deeper place in God's heart. This reality is at times hard to accept and understand. If one does not have a questioning nature, it can be frustrating and baffling to see another person resist even the most basic premises of our faith, such as the existence of God. However, if we do not learn to appreciate the potentially positive role of doubt in our own spiritual life, then we will be unable to relate credibly to the doubting Abrahams in our lives.

The Nature of Doubt

I like to think of a hike in the forest as an analogy for the role of doubt in the spiritual life. The hiker believes a path may lead to water; however, the way is unmarked and the person has never actually seen the water to be sure. The path comes to many forks and the hiker must choose which way to go. There are many ways to reach the water. At some points, spots in the path seem to lead away from the water. The hiker might take the way that veers off for different reasons. Some hikers lose faith that the path will lead to water, so they decide to try another way. Others see that the path leads away temporarily, but they keep to it, trusting that they will ultimately end up closer to the water than they were before.

In the same way, the path of life is meant to lead all of us to Christ, the Living Water. Some people take very creative paths to the water—they want to explore the forest, to know its nooks and crannies so they can discover for themselves the best place to end up in the forest. Other people stubbornly try to make their way as far from the water as possible, either because they dislike or have been hurt by other hikers headed in that direction or they do not even believe the water exists. Others accidentally stumble, through bad advice and poor direction, on a path leading away from the water without realizing it. Of course, even when a person knows he or she is stubbornly going the wrong way, as long as that person is alive there is the opportunity to turn around and get back on a path that leads to the water.

This analogy helps to illustrate the complicated nature of doubt. There are ways of doubting or struggling with the faith that are natural—what the *Catechism of the Catholic Church* calls "involuntary doubt"—and then there is the kind of doubt that is "voluntary," which is a "deliberately cultivated" doubt. Deliberate, willful doubt is sinful and can lead to "spiritual blindness," while involuntary doubt, if not cultivated, is not sinful in itself (see no. 2088). This may sound black and white—some ways of doubting are neutral and others are bad. However, there is rarely a clear place where one can look at a person and say with assurance that what the *Catechism* calls "natural doubt" has turned into "voluntary" doubt. This is why it is imperative for us to tread carefully when we meet with doubt in a loved one. God is the judge of our loved one's heart, not us. Even if we are absolutely convinced that a person's doubt has turned into a sinful, willful lack of belief, it still makes sense to compassionately try to meet the person at the point of pain that may have caused him or her to turn away from the faith rather than dwell on whether we personally think that person's doubt is sinful or not. Regardless of whether a loved one experiences natural or involuntary doubt, we can rest assured that God can use the paths our loved ones take for good; he can lead them back to the water—they may just end up taking a more scenic route!

God has a view from above the complicated maze of each individual's life path. He knows exactly where each person is headed, where they can make a right turn, and where they can head back to the water. Only he knows if a person's path away from the water is neutral and will end up at the water anyway, is positive and will lead the person close to the water, or is negative and will continue to lead away. We cannot see our own path clearly, let alone someone else's. Therefore, in view of the complexity of each person's spiritual journey of doubt and faith, it makes sense to stand in awe of the mystery and acknowledge our inability to know exactly what is going on in the midst of a person's doubt. It is impossible to make sure judgments about the nature of another person's spiritual journey. In the face of this uncertainty, we are invited to see each person's doubt, even when it seems to be of the most negative nature, as an opportunity to help the person find a path that, in the end, is closer to the water than when he or she started to question their faith.

Doubt, Reason, and Faith

In our modern world, people are encouraged to question virtually everything, even what has traditionally been accepted and revered as true. More and more people see it as a serious responsibility to search for answers to their questions and to reject their faith if they do not find satisfying responses.

Javier, a man who was away from the faith for many years, describes how his unanswered questions in high school ultimately led him to leave the Church:

My classes convinced me of how critical it is to question one's own upbringing and make decisions based on rational evidence rather than behave like automatons following the dictates of any particular leader or conforming to the standards set by a culture. My attitude toward Catholicism became more and more hesitant and defensive. I was afraid of being indoctrinated or brainwashed and not living up to the standards of critical thinking set in my classes.

I still had some contact with my religious friends and even sometimes attended a Catholic youth group. And while I now see the great value of the rituals and activities that the Catholic youth-group engaged in, they did not offer answers to the questions I was grappling with. Compared to my secular philosophy classes, my youth group activities in some ways felt like empty cheerleading and self-congratulating. Finally, I decided that since reason did not lead me to the conclusions of the Catholic faith, the only honest thing to do was to leave the Church.

Unfortunately, Javier's experience is similar to what many young people go through when they raise questions concerning their faith. Often, the very people who guide them in the faith are not prepared to answer their doubts. Or, unfortunately, it often happens that their questions are either not taken seriously or are responded to angrily. Without reasons to embrace the faith, these young people turn away, hurt and confused. If people who are natural doubters do not receive logical, sensitive, and calm responses to valid questions, they will most likely begin to look elsewhere for answers.

Rather than turning away the doubters in our lives, we can learn to face the doubts of others without fear and lead them through their doubt to God. In order to do this, it is important for us to first understand why Javier's approach, which is similar to many others who leave the Church, was not congruent with a life of faith.

In today's world, many people reject God or the Church because their reason does not lead them to the conclusions of the faith. This approach, although accepted by many people, including Catholics, is fundamentally flawed. Faith is not merely an intellectual exercise involving our human ability to reason. This does not mean that faith is unreasonable. God is Logos, or Reason itself, so to have faith in God is the most reasonable thing we can do. However, because we do not have God's knowledge and understanding, we have no way of comprehending the full reasonableness of our faith on own.

Just because we cannot understand something does not mean it is not reasonable or true. For example, a high school student may reject algebra as not being real simply because the student does not grasp it, but that does not mean that algebra is not real. Because we are human, we cannot rely solely on our limited ability to reason to bring us to the conclusions of faith. This is where the virtue of faith comes in. Faith allows us to leap beyond our reason; it helps us begin to fill the gap between our reason and God's reason. The very word we use for the body of knowledge that composes our religion—faith—demonstrates the necessity of this virtue. Because we are not God, without the virtue of faith it is impossible to accept the tenets of our faith.

When we understand the necessity of the virtue of faith in the process of accepting the faith, then doubt does not seem as intimidating or threatening. Doubt is a natural phenomenon in the nature of human existence. Our understanding of the faith can be, unsurprisingly, quite unclear; this lack of clarity comes from our being human and not God. Because we are not God, it is only natural that we will have doubts, areas where we will not understand. When we admit and accept our *own* sincere questions and doubts, we are able to connect with others in a way that is truly genuine and respectful, a way that will be listened to rather than ignored.

The opinions and perspectives of our loved ones may concern us and, if so, it is easy to become irritated or frustrated. It may be hard for us to understand why they think a certain way. Their questions and concerns, particularly about the faith, may seem cynical, skeptical, and negative. But we can learn to recognize our own questions in our loved ones' doubts and begin to see them in a more compassionate light, which will help us interact with them more effectively. When we are comfortable with the lack of certainty and understanding within ourselves, then we can become genuine and transparent witnesses of the faith for others.

If we understood God completely and had no questions, then what would be the point of the spiritual life? As Saint Augustine once said, "If you understood him, it would not be God."[2] Writer Marc Barnes puts it like this:

> In many ways, belief requires doubt. It is precisely the doubt I feel when I've looked at the Eucharist that makes my belief valid. It is the fact that the abyss opens up all around me, that the words "all lies" are whispered into my ears that makes belief possible.... If there were no doubt I would not be free to choose God, rather he would be forced upon me.[3]

Doubt is not the exclusive domain of non-believers and skeptics. Humble trust is the key attitude that differentiates a person with natural doubts who chooses to remain in the Church from someone who remains in their doubt and "deliberately cultivate[s]" it (*CCC*, no. 2088).

This is why it is so important to provide a model of faith for our loved ones that is not superficial in its lack of natural doubt. If people of faith try to appear to have it all together, then the doubters in their lives will most likely begin to gravitate away from the Church in a quest for understanding. But the truth is that in order to practice the virtue of faith, it is necessary to overcome difficulties in understanding in order to accept it. Even the Blessed Mother could be said to have experienced a moment of "involuntary doubt" or hesitation at the annunciation! We will not be free of confusion until heaven. By asking God to bring us in touch with the fears and doubts that may be far beneath our conscious faith, we show him that we desire to understand and be in communion with non-believers. We do not enter this communion to lose our faith; rather, through true empathy for others, we can be living proof that not understanding is not a reason to stop believing.

Accepting and Confronting Doubt with God

When we are faced with questions from someone who doubts the faith, it is normal to feel fearful that we will not know the answer. Often, our fear expresses itself in anger or defensiveness toward the person asking the question. We may feel this anger and anxiety when asked a question because we have not faced our own doubts. Our fear may be a sign of a lack of faith. But rejecting how we feel, or the person asking the question, will not solve the problem. Instead, we have to choose to walk with Jesus *through* our doubts in order to reach a place where we can begin to feel comfortable with our human weakness. It is likely we will never move beyond our doubts, at least not in this life, but we can come to a place where our uncertainties will not negatively impact our interactions with our skeptical loved ones.

We can learn to model a healthy relationship with doubt by living our doubts honestly, while at the same time holding them lightly. We hold our doubts lightly when we accept the reality of our questions, while also radically trusting in God, who helps us to have faith in him rather than our own perspectives. One of my atheist friends was shocked when I once said to him, "On a regular basis, I doubt that God exists." I was being honest; thoughts about

God's possible non-existence cross my mind quite often. I call them my "atheist flashbacks." They do not shake me like they used to; I don't dwell on them, but nevertheless I do experience these involuntary doubts. As Christians, we are not called to demonstrate false self-assurance to others; faith is not *self*-assurance, it is trust in God and in the assurance that *God* is trustworthy. With faith, we can face our doubt and trust its potential to bring us closer to Jesus. Struggles with doubt are often what mark milestones in our journey of faith. If we face our uncertainty head-on with trust in God, we can be confident that we will give our faith the opportunity to grow and to become more profound.

If we are not convinced that doubt can lead to a growth of faith with the help of God, we simply have to look to the Gospels for proof. Following the death of Jesus, the apostles were reeling from the violent and swift reversal of their expectations and plans. All of the apostles were filled with doubt after the crucifixion of Jesus, but Thomas was perhaps the most notorious doubter. After Jesus appeared to the other apostles, Thomas refused to believe their testimony and insisted: "Unless I see the mark of the nails in his hands, and put my finger in the mark of the nails and my hand in his side, I will not believe" (Jn 20:25). What is striking about Thomas's doubt is the intransigence of it; he gives no indication that his mind can be changed unless Jesus appears right in front of him. And, like a serious doubter, Thomas insists on material evidence; he must put his fingers into the wounds before he will believe.

Often, when this Gospel passage is discussed, Thomas is condemned for his doubting ways. But Jesus does not condemn Thomas. Instead, Jesus reminds Thomas to accept the gift of faith rather than wallow in his doubts. He gently chides him, "Do not doubt but believe" (20:27). In the same way, Jesus urges us all to let go of our doubts and put more faith in God than in ourselves. But

Jesus also recognized that Thomas, in his weakness, needed more. So Jesus invited Thomas to probe the wounds in his hands and side. It is not clear whether Thomas accepted the invitation. However, Thomas's response to Jesus's invitation to believe is recorded in Scripture, and it is perhaps one of the most revealing and beautiful phrases of wonder and worship: "My Lord and my God!" (20:28–29). With these words, Thomas the doubter becomes the first to understand the most central mystery of the Christian faith: Jesus is not only the Christ; he is also God. And so through the centuries believers repeat the words of Thomas, the apostle who faced his doubt with Jesus.

Is it a coincidence that the most obstinate doubter became the first apostle to recognize the true identity of Jesus as both God and man? I believe not. In his doubt, Thomas took a road away from the water, but he allowed Jesus to lead him back. This journey helped Thomas to recognize the deep spiritual mystery of the divinity and humanity of Jesus. Saint Gregory the Great goes so far as to declare: "The disbelief of Thomas has done more for our faith than the faith of the other disciples."[4] Thomas proves that if we honestly confront our doubts with openness to God's help, then our questions can bring us to understand deep spiritual realities.

The example of Thomas shows us that doubt can indeed play a positive role in our faith, but it is important to remember that doubt is only positive if it is ultimately overcome by faith. Jesus clearly urges his disciples to choose faith over doubt. In the Gospel of Mark he says, "If you do not doubt in your heart, but believe that what you say will come to pass, it will be done for you" (11:23). As people of faith, we are not called to pretend we do not have difficulty understanding some aspects of the faith. Rather, at the moment when doubt and faith do battle, Jesus calls us to believe, to choose faith. We choose faith not because our questions disappear, but because we prefer to rely on God's trustworthiness than on our own doubts. In the same way that Jesus urged Thomas, "Do not doubt but believe," we can urge our loved ones to choose faith over doubt, to choose God's vision over their own (see Jn 20:27).

An Attitude of Openness, Respect, and Compassion

We can only encourage our loved ones to choose faith over doubt if we adopt an attitude that welcomes questions in the first place. If we are open to questions, then chances are our loved ones will feel comfortable asking them. Dialogue is often more fruitful when it is initiated in freedom by the seeker rather than in response to something we say. It is clear in the Gospels that Jesus was open to questions, even responding to those obviously asked in bad faith. When the Pharisees and scribes tried to mix him up or get him to say the wrong thing, Jesus responded firmly, simply, and confidently. We can adopt his openness and respond to questions in the same way.

In order to get a person to ask a question, it helps to be open, but it is also key to continue this attitude throughout the conversation, even when it becomes heated or emotional. It is normal to feel defensive when we are faced with a question, especially if we do not know the answer. However, if we pause and ask the Holy Spirit for help, he will guide us. Jesus was full of the Spirit when he responded to others. For this reason, he was never fenced-in by their questions. Jesus did not feel obliged to respond exactly to what a person asked him. So often, if Jesus seemed to have a choice between answers A and B, his answer would be L, M, N, O, and P! In the same way, we are never duty-bound to answer the exact question we are asked. In fact, if we follow the example of Jesus, unexpected answers are perfectly acceptable and sometimes preferable. Jesus reached beyond the expected because God's way of thinking far surpasses our own. The Spirit can guide us beyond the superficial to unexpected answers; we have only to let go of the reins of the conversation and see where the Spirit leads.

You may now have a more positive view of the potential role of doubt in your loved one's life and feel better able to receive your loved ones' questions with peace. But you also may feel you need more specific guidance in how to respond to questions. First of all, realize that giving the right answer is not the most important thing. If we know the answer to a loved one's question, that's great. But knowing the answer can often play only a small part in bringing someone closer to God. *How* we answer a question is much more important.

Of course, if we do not know how to respond to our loved ones' questions, we can look for the answer ourselves or direct them to someone else. Your parish priest or a knowledgeable lay person you know may be able to help, or there are many resources online. But more importantly, we should avoid giving others the impression that our faith is simply about facts. Sure, our questions have factual answers. But we should always strive to direct the ones we love to dialogue with God. Prayer illuminates the darkness of doubt with the light of God. Prayer helps us to reason as God reasons. Prayer reveals that God is the ultimate answer to all questions. So, *whether we can answer a question or not*, we should always remember to urge others to talk directly to God in prayer, if they are open to that.

When loved ones ask us questions about the faith, they are making themselves vulnerable and, in some way, are unlocking the mystery of who they are before us. Because they may try to protect themselves in their vulnerability, questions can come across as challenging and angry. If someone comes across this way, we can still choose to respect that person's dignity by responding in a respectful way. Even if a person's question is so clearly off base that we cannot answer it, we can still take the person seriously. It helps to remember that no matter how or why a person asks a question, we can give thanks that he or she *is* asking a question because this provides an opportunity for dialogue. Their approach may be off-putting or downright rude, but with the help of the Holy Spirit we can respond without taking such things personally. It helps to remember that a person's aggressive approach may be coming from a place of hurt, the source of which we may not know, but the person deserves a compassionate response nevertheless. If we remain calm, and do not take personally the way a question is asked, we will be more likely to respond in a way that will be heard.

No matter the situation, it always helps to probe deeper into the place the person is coming from before trying to answer a question. Showing interest in our loved ones tells them that we take them seriously. When we focus on responding to the *person* rather than the exact question, we avoid jumping into long-winded answers that are not relevant to the person standing before us. If we are more focused on ourselves than on listening to the other person, we are likely to give a perfectly logical answer that might not be helpful at all in the person's search for truth. By asking questions and listening first, we may not be able to show off our knowledge of a particular subject, but we will be more likely to respond effectively.

Unfortunately, Christians do not always respond to questions respectfully or calmly, perhaps because many of us feel a need to communicate *facts* to our loved ones. But the truth is not just facts; it is not what we do (or do not) have stored in our brains from study. The Truth is a person. The Truth is Jesus and he is accessible to all, whether or not we have a PhD in theology. We are communicating the fullness of Truth only if we communicate with the love, peace, and humility of Christ. To respond to questions humbly, even to say "I don't know," can be a much more effective evangelizing moment than giving the right answer in the wrong way. Ultimately, the right answer without Christ-like delivery is not the right answer.

Even when we may have said all the right things, we should not be disappointed when the doubter walks away unsatisfied. Often, the deepest questions cannot be answered with words. Sometimes our disappointment may be a form of pride. If someone does not understand something more clearly after we have explained it to them, we may feel like we have failed. But if we judge the success of our interactions this way, we will almost always be disappointed. The central role in our loved one's conversion belongs to God, not to us. Doubters must work through their questions and experience for themselves God's light shining through the darkness of their doubt. This is a delicate and precious process, one that we should respect and never try to force. After we have answered a loved one's question, we have to ask God for the grace to let go and trust that God continues to walk with them in their doubt.

Conclusion

> "Then he became angry and refused to go in. His father came out and began to plead with him."
>
> — Luke 15:28

When the elder son returns one day from the fields, he finds a party being thrown for his irresponsible younger brother who has just returned after blowing his inheritance. The elder son is understandably angry, and he refuses to go into the house when he sees his father celebrating the return of his younger brother. He second-guesses his father's decision. The elder son doubts his father's love. The father's response to his elder son is very revealing. When his younger son demanded his share of the inheritance, the father did not say a word and "divided his property between them." The younger son demonstrated a kind of doubt that was willful and stubborn. And yet, the father did not yell or chastise; he was silent. But when the elder son shows his rebellious anger, the father comes out of the house and begins "to plead with him." The father reveals the divine response to different kinds of doubt in our loved ones' lives.

When a person is intransigent and resists hearing any other perspectives, as the prodigal son was when he demanded his inheritance, then we may be called to a silent witness of the faith. Although difficult, sometimes all we can do is watch mournfully as our loved ones walk away from the Father's house, and pray that someday they will be open to returning. But when someone is more honest in their doubts, not intent on rejecting the faith, and is open to feedback, then, like the father with the elder son, we are called to make the effort to "plead" with them. The Greek word for plead is *parakaleo*, and it is often used in the New Testament, especially by Saint Paul. *Parakaleo* can mean plead, but it can also mean exhort, instruct, urge, and encourage. The Father takes this stance toward honest doubters; he is not enraged by their questions, nor is he frustrated; he does not roll his eyes or sigh heavily in response to their hesitations. No, the Father responds to these kinds of doubts with encouragement, exhortations and humble pleas.

The detail that the father "came out" of the house may seem unimportant, but it reveals the father's humility. When we interact with doubters, we must be able to "come out" of the house of our preconceived ideas and firmly held beliefs. We do not leave truth behind, but we *are* called to face doubters with openness and acceptance, even when their views may come across as repugnant or belligerent. In our interactions with the doubters in our life, we are called to be like our heavenly Father—patient, compassionate, and open. Together with the Father, let us make the first step out of ourselves and toward those we love.

CHAPTER SEVEN

Why Our Faith Matters

"Having a sense of the Church is something fundamental for every Christian, every community, and every movement. It is the Church which brings Christ to me, and me to Christ; parallel journeys are very dangerous!" [1]

— Pope Francis

A practicing Catholic recently asked me why her stepchildren should be baptized. She seemed to understand it was important but couldn't explain why to her unconvinced husband. Sometimes we know in our gut that something is right. We know attending Mass is important. We know a relationship with God is key. We want our loved ones to enjoy the gifts of the Church. But we don't always know how to articulate our beliefs, much less defend them or explain them to others. This chapter is a little catechetical interlude that provides some of the nitty gritty reasons why actually *practicing* the faith really matters in an age when many people see nothing wrong with identifying themselves as "spiritual but not religious." Some of you may be familiar with the concepts I cover in this chapter. But even if you are, I hope that the way I articulate the importance of practicing the faith, particularly in relationship to your loved ones, will be helpful.

Ultimately our desire for loved ones to return to the Church is a desire for them to grow closer to God. The practical details in this chapter are just the background needed to help us understand more deeply why the institutional Church plays a role in our relationship with Jesus. Faith is not a private affair between God and me. The process of growing in union with God happens most clearly and surely in a sacramental faith community. The more we accept and understand this, the more clearly we can communicate it to our loved ones, not necessarily with words, but always with the joyous, brilliant light that comes from our own relationship with God, tended and cared for in the community of the Church.

The Church and Salvation

Many people today believe in God but see nothing wrong with declaring that they do not go to church. Even the word "religion" has become charged with negative connotations, evident in books, YouTube videos, and everyday conversations in which "religion" is disparaged. People who believe in God but claim not to believe in religion often insist that their faith is individual and deeply personal. This way of looking at our relationship with God has some truth. We each contain the shocking, matchless beauty of a masterpiece individually crafted by the Creator of our universe.

Like a treasure chest full of jewels, all people sparkle in a unique way when held up to the light of Christ. Because we are unique, we each relate to God differently.

However, despite our individuality, God designed a fundamental plan for the salvation of all human beings. The paramount way to relate to God is found in his plan for salvation, which is the fullest and most complete way that *all* humans can be in relationship with him. This way, paved with graces, is found in the Church. Salvation through the Church is paramount because God *designed and inhabits it* in the presence of Jesus in the Eucharist and in the members of the Church, the Body of Christ. Pope Francis, echoing the words of the Vatican II document *Dogmatic Constitution on the Church,* writes: "The Church is sent by Jesus Christ as the sacrament of the salvation offered by God."[2]

It may seem arrogant to claim that God's plan for salvation is found in a specific religion. These days, any claim to truth can sound arrogant to our modern ears. But then, should we also think Jesus was arrogant for claiming to be God? In the same way, it is not arrogant to claim that the Church is the presence of God in the world and contains God's perfect plan of salvation. Jesus himself told us that building a church was part of his earthly mission: "And I tell you, you are Peter, and on this rock I will build my church" (Mt 16:18). The Church is the perfect, mysterious, irreplaceable, exquisite invention of God. It is, of course, important to keep in mind that we, the humans who make up the Church, are not perfect. We are flawed, sinful, and imperfect in many ways; in fact we are often a downright embarrassment and scandal compared to the ideal of God's beautiful plan for salvation in the Church. But, despite our sin, God is nevertheless active and alive within the Church. And *he* is perfect.

If God meant for faith to be an individual experience outside of the context of a larger community, he would have designed salvation another way. However, God wants our salvation and our sanctification to happen in community, within the worldwide Church. He did this because ultimately we are meant for union with him. But how can we understand union with God if we have not first lived it on earth with our brothers and sisters? Unity is found in the Church; therefore God provides special graces within the bounds of the Church. God designed a way for us to be in union with our brothers and sisters and in relationship with him. It would be a betrayal of his love that unfolds for us in this plan to refuse to recognize God's love as it is expressed in the Church.

God's plan for salvation includes Baptism, the foundation of Christian relationship with God. But it also includes much more: the Real Presence of Jesus in the Eucharist, Reconciliation or Confession, the other sacraments, the Communion of the Saints, the intercession of Mary, the teaching authority of the Magisterium, and the list goes on and on. What other faiths may consider superfluous or unnecessary is rather a sign of the abundance of gifts God has given us in the Church for our salvation and sanctification. God has given us these treasures in order to lead us to greater union with *the* Treasure, namely him.

In other words, in the Church, God provides a person with the surest path for salvation and for growth in holiness. This is the crux of why it is important for our loved ones to return to the Church. If someone feels very little motivation to invite their loved ones to the Church, it might be because they don't realize the central importance of the Church's role in our salvation. Others may want their loved ones to return to the practice of the faith but find it difficult to accept or communicate that God's plan for salvation is most perfectly present in the Church. And still others may communicate this truth in a way that does not reflect the beauty of God's plan, and so their message is not well-received. Wherever we find ourselves in this regard, I hope it will be helpful to explore some of the reasons why practicing our faith matters. The more clearly we understand the importance of our faith, the more compelling our invitations to loved ones will be.

Baptism and Salvation

Saint Paul exhorted the Corinthians to remember their baptism and his reminder is still relevant today: "Do you not know that you are God's temple and that God's Spirit dwells in you?" (1 Cor 3:16). Baptism is the most important way a relationship with God and with the Church is initiated. Baptism is the primary life source and foundation of every Christian's relationship with God. When Jesus died on the cross, the Gospel of John tells us, "one of the soldiers pierced his side with a spear, and at once blood and water came out" (19:34). Saint John Chrysostom, an early Church Father, wrote: "Beloved, do not pass over this mystery without thought; it has yet another hidden meaning, which I will explain to you. I said that water and blood symbolized Baptism and the holy Eucharist."[3] Although the earthly life of Jesus has ended, his presence is still with us in the Eucharist and through the gift of our Baptism.

When we are baptized, the Holy Trinity comes to dwell *within* us. We may know this aspect of our faith intellectually, but many Christians have not taken this truth to heart. Through our Baptism, we have been given the amazing privilege of becoming God-bearers. Like Mary, we become living tabernacles of the Trinity. This is an astounding reality. If we could all come to understand more deeply the power of this mystery, our world would be a different place. Wherever we go, God goes with us, not in a poetic, symbolic way, but God *really dwells within* us through our Baptism. We are his home, his dwelling place, his Temple. This indwelling of the Trinity is the most essential gift of the faith Jesus has left us.

Scripture clearly tells us that the gift of Baptism is not symbolic or a superfluous trapping, it is indispensable. In the Gospel of John, Jesus reveals the mystery of the indwelling to his apostles when he tells them: "Those who love me will keep my word, and my Father will love them, and we will come to them and make our home with them" (14:23). Both the Gospels of Matthew and Mark conclude with Jesus exhorting the disciples to proclaim the Gospel *and to baptize.* Jesus says: "Go therefore and make disciples of all nations, baptizing them in the name of the Father and of the Son and of the Holy Spirit" (Mt 28:19; see Mk 16:16). Baptism is so essential that the Church teaches it is necessary for salvation. Jesus himself states this when he tells Nicodemus: "Very truly, I tell you, no one can enter the kingdom of God without being born of water and Spirit" (Jn 3:5).

In her wisdom, the Church recognizes that not all those who enter heaven have received a Christian baptism by water. The Church acknowledges two other possible kinds of baptism, the baptism of desire and the baptism of blood, or martyrdom. Those who desire to live a life in union with God, but do not understand the importance of Baptism or fail to receive it through no fault of their own, can still be saved. As the *Catechism* explains: "It may be supposed that such persons would have *desired Baptism explicitly* if they had known its necessity" (no. 1260). The same is true for those who die for the faith before being baptized; they receive a baptism through the blood of their martyrdom. Again, the *Catechism* describes this mystery beautifully: "God has bound salvation to the sacrament of Baptism, *but he himself is not bound by his sacraments*" (no. 1257, emphasis added). In other words, Baptism is essential, but our merciful God has the final word.

Nevertheless, Scripture and Tradition both make it clear that Baptism is non-negotiable to our faith, which is why we should be concerned if we have loved ones who are not baptized or who have neglected their Baptism through serious sin. Baptism is necessary for salvation. If our loved ones are not baptized, it is still possible, although more difficult, for them to be saved. But something this fundamental should not simply be presumed. In the same way, if our loved ones have seriously neglected their Baptism, and may be in a state of mortal sin, this again is reason for concern. God has designed a plan for our salvation and it happens through the grace of our Baptism. We should not allow ourselves to be overcome by anxiety over this; we have a merciful God. But we also should strive to take Baptism seriously and avoid shrugging it off as if it were something merely figurative and not a spiritual reality that deserves our attention, awe, and care. The saving grace that God desires us to receive through Baptism and the other sacraments is *very* important.

The Power of Sanctifying Grace

You may be concerned about your loved ones because you know the Church teaches that a person who commits a mortal sin loses sanctifying grace and the indwelling of the Trinity within them. It is true that the Trinity departs from the soul of someone who has committed mortal sin. Mortal sin is a person's way of telling God he is not welcome in their soul. So, God politely departs. However, it is important to keep this truth in perspective.

Our loved ones may be objectively involved in serious sin; however, no one but God knows for certain whether a person is guilty of a mortal sin. The *Catechism* tells us that "mortal sin is sin whose object is grave matter and which is also committed with full knowledge and deliberate consent" (no. 1857). We may think our loved ones know better; we may believe they know something to be true, but we can never know for sure what they truly understand in their hearts. Even the person who has committed a sin is often unable to say later whether they were fully aware of the seriousness of the sin or not. Only God knows objectively and truthfully what guides our hearts and how much we are aware of when we commit a serious sin. Indeed, many of the holiest people cannot say for certain what the state of their soul is before God. Saint Joan of Arc, when asked by her interrogators whether or not she was in a state of grace, responded, "If I am not, may God place me there; if I am, may God so keep me."[4]

So, we can never say for sure that the Trinity has departed from the soul of a person. It always makes sense to hope that the Trinity continues to dwell within the souls of our loved ones. Even if we knew for sure that those we love had lost the indwelling of the Trinity through sin, we could still cling to the knowledge that a baptized person is always a baptized person and God never departs from anyone's life. A person may reject the grace of Baptism, but grace does not disappear from one's life because God does not disappear from their life. God can give a person grace with or without Baptism. However, Baptism is the primary source, foundation, and conduit for God's grace in the spiritual life. Through the grace of the other sacraments, a person's baptismal union with God increases. If the baptismal presence is not there, there is no union that the other sacraments can increase.

You may ask why this is relevant to your loved ones if there is no way to know whether or not a person has lost the indwelling of the Trinity. What is important to understand is that when any person commits sin, mortal or venial, that person begins to strain or, in the case of mortal sin, completely ruptures one's baptismal relationship with God. This is true for everyone—for you and for me and for all of our loved ones. However, *the Church is the setting* that provides the ways to repair this relationship. After a person is baptized, the Church does not fade into the background, unneeded and unnecessary. Instead, the Church continually provides the sacraments, which are like a salve that heals the effects of original sin, the glue that repairs and strengthens our relationship with God, and the tinder that stokes the fire of our Baptism. For example, the sacrament of Reconciliation is vital in the practice of our faith because it actually *restores* the baptismal presence of the Trinity in the soul of any person in a state of mortal sin. If we are not in a state of mortal sin, the sacraments provide sanctifying grace that, if we cooperate, makes our union with God stronger and helps us to avoid sin. If we want the Trinitarian fire to burn, and to burn ever more brightly within our loved ones, they need to frequent the sacraments; they need to practice the faith.

Baptism Sticks with Us

Often when people leave the Church, they refer to themselves as "recovering Catholics." This phrase, usually meant as a joke or a hint of the pain at the root of their departure, also reveals the power of God present in the Catholic faith, and particularly the power of Baptism. Our loved ones may become inactive in their faith for a time or formally disassociate themselves from the Church, but Baptism sticks with them:

> Incorporated into Christ by Baptism, the person baptized is configured to Christ. Baptism seals the Christian with *the indelible spiritual mark* (character) of his belonging to Christ. *No sin can erase this mark*, even if sin prevents Baptism from bearing the fruits of salvation. (CCC, no. 1272, emphasis added)

Baptism marks us forever. No matter what our loved ones do, what they get involved in, what sins they commit, they are marked; they belong to God. Even if a person commits a mortal sin, he or she still remains baptized, marked by God as his adopted son or daughter. This is not some kind of symbolic change; it is a deep, ontological change. Baptized people are new creations; they belong to God as adopted sons and daughters. Baptism's effect on us perhaps explains why many former Catholics cannot seem to shake the feeling that something stays with them, even when they reject their faith.

By Baptism we are also incorporated into the priesthood of Christ, which enables us to take part in Christian worship. Whether a person knows it or not, Baptism makes each of us a part of the Body of Christ. If a person is in sin, he or she is not cut off from the Body of Christ. A person may be a temporarily dead part of the Body, but, by virtue of Baptism, that person remains part of the Body nevertheless. This is why Catholics often feel somehow at home at the Mass, even when they have been away for years. All of this is important to remember because we can sometimes give too much credence to outward reality rather than to far more important spiritual realities. Our baptized loved ones belong to Christ no matter what is currently happening in their lives. The mark of Baptism is an imprint on their souls that can never be erased. This baptismal mark aches in our loved ones, reminding them that something is missing, calling them home.

Communicating the Beauty of the Church

We want others to know God and to live in relationship with him so they can continue that relationship in heaven. This is why we are called to participate in the Church's mission of evangelization, to proclaim the Gospel to the world. The Church's teachings on grace and salvation that we have been discussing can be thought of as the skeleton of evangelization. If grace were not found in Jesus who resides in the Church, our evangelization would be for naught. In other words, the impetus of our evangelization is founded in our belief that Jesus and his graces are most fully revealed within the life of the Church.

It may be difficult for you to imagine communicating God's plan of salvation in the Church to your loved ones. It is important to gauge, with the help of the Spirit's inspiration, whether they are open to hearing this truth. We often barrage others with truths that do not meet them where they are. If our loved ones do not believe in God, it might be wise not to hammer them with ideas about salvation in the Church. For someone who does not believe in God, the very concept of salvation will be completely foreign to their worldview. In the Letter to the Hebrews, the teaching of God is compared to "solid food" (5:14). However, some people are only ready for "softer" truths, as the letter states: "You need someone to teach you again the basic elements of the oracles of God. You need milk, not solid food" (5:12). Some people are not ready to hear about the role of the Church in our salvation because they may not even believe that God loves them or that he exists. Many of our loved ones need a very gradual introduction, or reintroduction, to the faith, beginning with the basics.

Sometimes the best thing we can do is to encourage our loved ones in their spiritual practice, whatever it may be. In college I brought my parents to a Quaker meeting. I was not sure how they would react. I hoped they would be proud that I was doing something spiritual, but I secretly assumed they would be unhappy with me. I was not ready for their reaction. My mother describes the experience:

> I remember sitting at a Quaker service with my daughter, tears streaming down my face. I was so grateful to God for this simple, unassuming religion where there were so few barriers to cause my confused and angry girl to stub her toe. Here she could find a sense of peace and spiritual connection that she couldn't

find in the Church, where she had experienced so much hurt. Several years earlier I would have been so upset if I knew she was interested in being a Quaker. Now I rejoiced. So much had happened since those days—in her heart and mine. Instead of my heart being closed to any other option than Catholicism for my children, I yearned for any sign of Theresa's openness to God.

There will probably be times when your loved ones will not be open at all to returning to the Catholic Church. They may find community and spiritual nourishment in a Christian group that is not Catholic. These communities, particularly because they follow Jesus, have much truth in them. The *Dogmatic Constitution on the Church* puts it this way: "[The] Church constituted and organized in the world as a society, subsists in the Catholic Church ... although many elements of sanctification and of truth are found outside of its visible structure."[5] In other words, communities outside of the visible bounds of the Church can still help lead others to Christ.

Some of your loved ones may begin to explore other spiritual avenues outside of Christianity, even Eastern practices. We certainly need caution in our approach to this reality; real dangers lurk in the New Age Movement and in unhealthy spiritual communities. But when our loved ones are doing something that brings them closer to God, in whatever setting, this is usually preferable to a life lived without any connection to the Lord. When God sees that a person's heart is more open to other avenues of communication, he may try to meet the person there before gently leading him or her to the fullness of truth in the Church. Our reactions to a loved one's exploration of another faith, if too negative, can reveal a desire to control and, more than that, even a lack of faith. As believers, we are called to believe in the power of God who can work through *all* things.

However, we do have a responsibility to share with our loved ones the beauty of salvation within the Church, wherever they might be in their spiritual journey. We do this with words if possible, but sometimes we are called to communicate it in other ways, namely by the witness of our lives. Always respecting where our loved ones are, and following the inspirations of the Spirit, we can witness to the wonder of our faith through our love for God and others. Our faith speaks when we live it to the fullest, when we abandon ourselves to God's plan of salvation for our own lives. And sometimes, even in the least likely circumstances, we may be called to share in words how important the Church is for our salvation. When this time comes, we should not be afraid; if we are following inspiration and show respect to our loved ones, we should not waver or step back. God will be with us.

You may fear that you will communicate this "hard" truth in a way that will turn your loved ones off. This is where the bare bones of truth need the flesh and tissue of joy and love that will breathe life into what we communicate and make it attractive. We cannot convey the importance of the Church effectively without joy or love. Pope Paul VI exhorts us:

> Let us therefore preserve our fervor of spirit. Let us preserve the delightful and comforting joy of evangelizing, even when it is in tears that we must sow. . . . May the world of our time, which is searching, sometimes with anguish, sometimes with hope, be enabled to receive the Good News not from evangelizers who are dejected, discouraged, impatient, or anxious, but from ministers of the Gospel whose lives glow with fervor, who have first received the joy of Christ, and who are willing to risk their lives so that the kingdom may be proclaimed and the Church established in the midst of the world.[6]

Joy is so fundamental; it is the key to evangelization. Joy is particularly vital when it comes to communicating the reality of the Church's role in our salvation. If we communicate the importance of the Church for salvation without joy, we betray the beautiful truth we are called to reveal with our lives. The abundance of grace available in the Church is a cause for joy, and *from* this joy we communicate that truth to others. In his apostolic exhortation, *The Joy of the Gospel* (*Evangelii Gaudium*) Pope Francis laments that "there are Christians whose lives seem like Lent without Easter."[7] Rather than presenting the faith with joy, some Christians confront others with anger, glumness, and disdain. Pope Francis pleads with us to try another way, to experience the exhilarating joy of salvation in our own lives so that we may communicate it to others. He writes:

> Christians have the duty to proclaim the Gospel without excluding anyone. Instead of seeming to impose new obligations, they should appear as people who wish to share their joy, who point to a horizon of beauty and who invite others to a delicious banquet.[8]

Conclusion

"He squandered his property."

— Luke 15:13

The prodigal son squandered the gift of his father's property. In some translations of this phrase, the Greek word for property, *ousia*, is translated "inheritance." The literal meaning of the word *ousia* is "what one has."[9] When we consider what the prodigal son had, it is easy to see that, more than wealth, the most valuable thing he squandered was his relationship with the Father, with God. If the prodigal son represents all of us, we can see that the "inheritance" he receives is like our baptismal inheritance. In the Letter to Titus, we are told that God poured the Holy Spirit on us "through Jesus Christ our Savior, so that, having been justified by his grace, we might become heirs according to the hope of eternal life" (3:6–7). Through the death of Jesus, we are sons and daughters, and, hence, heirs of God the Father, and the riches of grace available to us through the Church are our inheritance.

We receive the indwelling of the Trinity and become part of the continuing presence of God through the Church at the moment of our Baptism. But this "inheritance" of grace that we receive, through the death of Jesus on the cross, is something that can easily be thrown away, as the tale of the Prodigal Son demonstrates. God calls us to care for and nourish the baptismal treasure of our faith. The Prodigal Son shows us that we, along with our loved ones, can easily squander the riches God gives us in the sacramental life of the Church. God does not control how we use his gifts; he gives them to us freely. It is up to us whether we receive and make good use of the Father's grace or waste it completely. For ourselves and for our loved ones, let us pray that we may cherish our Baptism and nourish it with the continuing grace of God's presence in the Eucharist and in the sacrament of Reconciliation. May we all grow to understand and appreciate the presence of God in the Church and in ourselves.

CHAPTER EIGHT

Respecting Free Will

"I have wandered through even the deepest chamber of all the prisons of all those who, in despair, have struggled against God's freedom." [1]

— Hans Urs von Balthasar

———◇◇◇———

A fter I returned to the Church, I became frustrated with friends and family who did not understand the treasure I had newly rediscovered. I was not sure how to communicate with them, stay in relationship with them, or even love them, now that our worldviews had so little in common. I was surprised at my controlling, judgmental, and uncharitable attitude, especially because I had been in their shoes just months before! I knew that my approach was not helpful. I did not want to interact in this way with the people I loved, and I knew my behavior would not persuade them to think about returning to the Church. If anything, it pushed them even further away.

One day I was thinking about a particular person whose life decisions were of great concern to me. I knew my attachment to the situation was getting to be too much, so I called my mom and asked, "How did you do it? When I was really going off the deep end, how did you stay in relationship with me, love me, and help me feel accepted?" She paused for a moment and then responded, "Over time, God helped me to realize just how much he respects our ability to make our own decisions. He gives us free will, even though he knows that it brings great evil into the world. He respects our autonomy so much that he even allows us to make the terrible choice to separate ourselves from him forever. You were an adult and already knew how I felt about you being away from the Church. Beyond sharing my feelings, I realized that I had no right to force you to see things my way, no matter how concerned I was about your behavior."

At some point in life, we all learn, some later than others, that trying to control others is not effective. Spouses learn that control plays no part in love. Friends learn that control has no place in a relationship of mutuality. Even parents, though able to control their children's exterior actions for a short time, learn quickly that when their children become adults, they have little control over what they do. This is a good thing. We are not little gods, and the real God does not ask us to control other people. He asks parents to raise their children in the faith and to love them, but he does not ask parents to manipulate or force their kids to conform to their ideas, even if they are good ideas! He asks friends to caution, advise, and love one another, but he does not ask them to dominate or give orders. God never asks us to be something that even he, as Creator of the universe, is not.

The Gift and Burden of Free Will

Free will is a central paradox of our faith. It is a gift God has given us so that we may freely love him. Because we have free will, we are able to choose between actions that bring us closer to God and those that take us away from God. The *Catechism* puts it this way: "Human freedom is a force for growth and maturity in truth and goodness; it attains its perfection when directed toward God" (no. 1732). Because free will, by necessity, allows us to choose both good and evil, we can either choose to love God and grow in freedom or we can turn away from God and become enslaved by sin.

Sin is slavery because when we turn away from God, we can only turn in on ourselves. Without even realizing it, we easily end up centering our lives on ourselves rather than God. We may be completely unaware that we are living a self-centered life, because outwardly it can look like we are focused on God. We may go to church, pray, and be involved in many parish activities, but if we are not willing to let God guide us in the actual details of our lives, then ultimately we are centered on ourselves, not God. It is easy to assume we know God and what he wants, but often we only end up following our own concept of God's will for our lives. We can make ourselves the center of our lives through what seem like very small, unimportant choices in our day—when we put our own needs first, when we assume our desires and wants are more important than those of others. This kind of life, cut off from God's will, is not rooted in humility, the attitude foundational to faith. When we are not rooted in faith, we are likely to become more and more involved in ourselves, and gradually we become enslaved by our self-absorption. Sin is nothing more than slavery to our worst self.

Today, the idea of sin as slavery to ourselves is not commonly heard because our modern society has lost a sense of sin. Focusing on ourselves is not seen as sinful but rather normal, acceptable, and even to some extent a sign of psychological health in an independent person. Our modern world understands addiction, but not so much sin. However, if we understand the danger of addiction, we are on the way to understanding sin, as the two are closely related. If we are prideful, we often are addicted to affirmation. If we are gluttonous, we may be addicted to eating. If we are lustful, we can become addicted to pornography. The list goes on and on. In modern society we do not think of such things as offenses against God, but we do recognize that when they become obsessive, they can negatively affect our ability to live happy lives. As a society we may not use the word "sin," but we do acknowledge the potential for enslavement inherent in these activities, which is at least a start!

What does freedom mean, if not freedom from enslavement to sin? Jesus came to earth to set us free from the prison of sin. Saint Paul tells us: "For freedom Christ has set us free. Stand firm, therefore, and do not submit again to a yoke of slavery" (Gal 5:1). Jesus not only won for us salvation, he also won for us an abundance of grace that makes a life of freedom possible. We cannot completely escape from sin in this earthly life, but Jesus's death became a font of grace for us in our daily battle against sin. This freeing grace enables us to live evermore in union with God, the source of true freedom. So, free will gives us a choice. We can live a life unconcerned by our enslavement, our addiction to sin, or we can live a life that turns from sin and allows God to transform us to live in the freedom of his love.

When we surrender our will to God, this is, paradoxically, when we can truly begin to live in freedom. Without God's guidance, we easily center our lives on ourselves and fall into sin. But as Christians, we are called to live true freedom, to use our free will to submit ourselves to God in order to live in his freedom. When we relate to God in this way, we are freed from self-obsession, and we allow him not only to help us become free from sin, but also to become more like him. To truly live freely, we have to give up the false idea that freedom is found in living a life unfettered by obedience to anyone and completely directed by our own desires. Freedom lies not in doing what we please, but in doing what God pleases. It is not about making our own choices but in surrendering our choices to God so that we can love more deeply, give of ourselves, and communicate to others the breathtaking freedom of life in God. Our joyful lives centered on God can give those around us an example of the benefits of living in the freedom of God, and perhaps entice them to begin using their free will in a new way.

Responsibility to Share the Faith

If we fall into the world's way of seeing things, we may look at our loved ones' choice to leave the Church as an exercise in freedom. And they certainly are exercising their *free will*, but not their freedom. Our culture is very focused on freedom as freedom of choice. We hear the message that it is good to have a choice, period. However, freedom is a much broader, wider reality. We are only truly free when we make *good* choices; good choices allow us to experience the freedom of being in God. For example, a person may freely choose to eat junk food for every meal. Such a person is exercising free will, but this person's choices do not lead to what is best for him or her, so this action does not lead to greater freedom. To put it another way, God gives us a means to be free, our free will. If we use our free will to make good choices and grow closer to God who is good, then we can truly be free. True freedom can only be exercised in union with God.

If we understand freedom in this way, it helps us to see our loved ones' situations with more clarity. When those we love make decisions that bring them away from the ultimate good of Jesus fully present in the Church, it can only have a negative impact on their freedom. This is not to say that other Christians, or even non-Christians, are necessarily any less free, but the opportunity and the grace for living a life of freedom in God is fullest in the Church. It is also true that insofar as one willfully rejects the Church, one turns away from the freedom found in the unity and the fullness of truth within it.

So, the greatest opportunity for our loved ones to find freedom is within the Church, with the help of God's presence in the sacraments. If we truly understand the transformative power of the Eucharist and the other sacraments received after Baptism, then it only makes sense that we will long for our loved ones to experience it as well. However, when we strongly desire the graces in the Church for our loved ones, we may act in a way that is not respectful of their capacity to make free choices. We do this when we try to control or manipulate others to make the choices we want.

Manipulation is probably the most obvious way to impose on another person's free will, and we will look at this more closely later in the chapter. But there is perhaps an even more common and equally dangerous way we can disrespect our loved ones' freedom: namely, by never presenting others with the reasons why they should return to the Church. A policy of non-engagement infringes on a person's freedom in another way different from manipulation. Imagine a person who is voluntarily locked in a cage and seems quite happy to be there. Wouldn't it be absurd to say no one should talk to the caged person about how lovely the world outside the cage is because that would somehow disrespect the freedom of that person? In today's world, we can feel like we are imposing when we share our faith, but this attitude stems from an incorrect view of freedom. By sharing our faith with our loved ones, we show that we respect and love them enough to want that person to be *truly* free. Freedom is found in God. If we love someone, we want them to find true freedom in the salvific power of Jesus in the Church.

In the apostolic exhortation *Evangelization in the Modern World* (*Evangelii Nuntiandi*), Pope Paul VI tells us that the Church "exists in order to evangelize."[2] Laity have access to the people on the outer edges of the Church who may not be as open to receiving the faith from a priest—or anyone officially associated with the Church, for that matter. Vatican II, especially in its *Decree on the Apostolate of the Laity* (*Apostolicam Actuositatem*), emphasized the special role of the laity in the evangelization of the culture. We are not only called to share the Gospel with our families, but also with other members of the human family. When we see people who have fallen away from the Church, including our loved ones, we cannot simply hope that someone else will share the Good News with them. Evangelization is our duty and responsibility as Christians. It is the work of the entire Church.

We all share in the evangelizing mission of the Church, no matter who we are or how unimportant we think we might be. If we have found the power of God's grace in the sacraments and we believe Jesus is alive in the Church, we have a responsibility to share the treasure we have found with those we love. We are not obliged to make others accept the gifts offered through the Church, but we are asked to share the Good News with open, gentle hands. When we present the Gospel in this way, we risk God's gift being rejected with disdain, but it is a risk well worth taking if we realize that our words may play a role in our loved ones' return.

You may be thinking, "I am not articulate enough, I am not smart enough, I am not brave enough to evangelize my own family, let alone the culture!" We must not forget that our role in the Church's mission is not a burden; it will naturally flow out of our relationship with God. The work of salvation is not up to us. Jesus is our Savior. But God *does* desire to use us, in ways we may never have imagined. The more we love God, the more we allow him to transform us, the more we will evangelize, with our words *and* with our lives.

Our evangelization can take many forms. We do not have to write articles or stand on street corners (unless God calls us to that). We do not have to do great things to evangelize. But we do need to love, and to *be* love in the Church. When we love God, we will naturally extend this love to others and this love will attract souls to the freedom of Christ in the Church. As Pope Francis underscores in *The Joy of the Gospel*: "If we have received the love which restores meaning to our lives, how can we fail to share that love with others?"[3] So, be brave. Share your faith with your loved ones; they deserve to hear about the treasure you have found.

Sharing Without Compelling

Recognizing our responsibility to share our faith, it is also important to keep in mind that sharing is not compelling. Granted, it is certainly important for our loved ones to return to the Church, but we overstep our bounds when we try to force or impose our will on them through our actions, words, or manner of relating. God does not coerce, he invites. Archbishop Emeritus of San Francisco, George H. Niederauer, put it this way: "Christian belief in human freedom recognizes that we are called *but not compelled* by God to choose constantly the values of the Gospel (emphasis added)."[4] When we act in a way that puts psychological pressure on our loved ones to return to the Church, not because they have found the truth but because they want to please us, we can be sure we have encroached unjustly on their freedom and dignity.

If we desire to imitate God's love, it pays to reflect on God's profound respect for our loved ones' free will. God's love comes at no cost. He does not require us to love him or to see things his way before he loves and accepts us. He also does not require us to be perfect or sinless before we can receive his love. By approaching us in this way, God makes possible a love between him and his creatures that is all the more deep, free, and profound. If we respond to God's love without the slightest hint of compulsion, then his love is able to freely enter and transform us.

This is the same kind of love we are called to have for our loved ones; a love that invites, but does not force. Pope Francis does not mince words when he says that we cannot declare the Gospel "with inquisitorial beatings of condemnation"; instead, the Gospel must be "preached gently, with fraternity and love."[5] Therefore, we are called to model a love that proposes not imposes. This is the love of God. God invites, encourages, attracts, and proposes. He does not force, manipulate, or strong-arm anyone into accepting and loving him. As Saint John Paul II affirms in *Mission of the Redeemer*: "The Church addresses people with full respect for their freedom. Her mission does not restrict freedom but rather promotes it. *The Church proposes; she imposes nothing.*"[6]

Staying in Relationship

In order to propose the freedom of living in God to those we love, we need to be in relationship with them. Respect for our loved ones' free will is key to maintaining relationship. God does not cease his relationship with us when we make mistakes or walk away from him. He continues knocking at our door, trying to draw us back to him, and he asks you and me to do the same. Even when our loved ones' decisions make our stomachs churn and anxiety levels rise, God asks us to continue to remain in relationship.

When I was away from the Church, my parents never cut off contact with me, although they made it clear that they strongly disagreed with my behavior. I also never ceased contact with my parents because I knew they loved and accepted me, no matter what. Even if I were still away from the Church, continuing in self-destructive behavior, I know they would continue to love me. The love they showed me was not a codependent, weak, enabling love. Rather, it was a Christ-like love; they were open and honest about how they thought I should make different decisions, while at the same time making it clear that their love was not contingent on certain behavior of mine.

If our love for others is contingent rather than unconditional, it will most likely lead to a breakdown in our relationship with the person. The root of the difficulty often lies in a lack of respect for the free will of the person we love. We may disrespect another's free will through manipulation, for example, by ceasing contact as a kind of punishment. Or we may show constant displeasure with the person, believing our disapproval will change him or her. When we fall into manipulative tactics, we can be sure that this typically ineffective behavior grows out of a desire to control another person, which does not come from love. God does not control or try to control us. Although it certainly can be said that God doggedly pursues our souls, he does so in complete respect for our free will. God desires us to love him freely. Manipulation is often less about God and more about wanting another person to comply with our demands.

Of course, we should not tolerate dangerous behavior or choices that negatively impact our own lives. This can happen when the people we love are addicts or may be involved in other behaviors that can lead to serious boundary crossing. Such situations call for assertive and straightforward communication. If a person infringes on our rights with bad behavior, it is appropriate and necessary to set boundaries and limits, even if these boundaries involve a break in relationship for a time. But if we must break contact with a loved one due to the person's destructive behavior, this decision should also be made from love. We can always make it clear that our love for the person will never end, even if we are cutting ourselves off from him or her for a time out of respect for ourselves and our own freedom.

Acting from a place of real love and a desire for the person to find true freedom ensures that we will not enable bad behavior, on the one hand, or try to force a person to see things our way on the other. We can disrespect a person's freedom and damage our relationships if we try to control other people, but we can also do the same by becoming so enmeshed in their lives that we actually end up enabling or encouraging their bad behavior. If we stay in relationship with our loved ones but encourage sinful behavior with our support—monetary, emotional, or otherwise—this can also be an affront to true freedom. Making an effort to reach the balance between these two extremes will likely enable us to remain in a healthy relationship with our loved ones and influence them positively. It will not be easy—it never is—but when we relate to our loved ones with God as our model, he will show us the way.

If we long for our loved ones to live in the freedom of God, we must strive first to live true Christian freedom ourselves. When we find ourselves struggling with either tendency, to control or to enable, our positive motivation to work on these points can come from the knowledge that our loved ones need us, not as we are but holy, as God is able to make us. Only by striving to live in the true freedom of God can we convincingly invite our loved ones to participate in this freedom. However, in order to encourage someone to experience God's freedom in an authentic way we must respect that person's free will and always invite rather than coerce.

The Power of Silence

After I reached adulthood while still away from the Church, my parents wisely chose to engage with me on issues of faith only when it really mattered. When I had been a minor in high school, they had insisted on the fundamentals. But at a certain point, I received the clear message from my parents that I was an adult, responsible for my own actions. This recognition of my free will gave me more pause than anything else they had done to influence my behavior. My parents realized that it did not pay to vainly attempt to control me. Instead, they validated the good things that I did and maintained a strategic silence otherwise. When we are in relationships with people who are away from the Church, an important way to respect their free will and to respect them as persons is to use silence strategically. In other words, we can choose to speak to our loved ones about issues of faith or challenge them, but it is most effective and respectful when we do so irregularly and without undue pressure.

My parents' silence must have been incredibly difficult for them, but it was effective because it was a silence of strategy, not timidity. They spoke to me about issues of faith and challenged me when the Spirit moved them. They spoke briefly, clearly, and irregularly. One instance in particular remains in my memory. After I graduated from college I decided to move in with my boyfriend. He and I visited my family before the move, and my mom asked if she could speak to us. She said, "I have to be really honest with both of you. I am very disappointed that you are moving in together and I do not agree with your decision. I do not think it will be good for your relationship. And whether you believe it or not, it is wrong to live together before marriage. You are not respecting yourselves and you are not respecting God." You could have heard a pin drop. I was ashamed and embarrassed.

My mother's words struck deep because she knew how to couch her statements with silence so they would resound powerfully in my conscience. If my mom had made comments like this to me regularly, I may have just ignored her or rolled my eyes. Instead, she spoke to me when necessary, but otherwise surrounded her words with silence and love. I felt accepted by both of my parents, even though they disagreed with my actions, and this is part of what made their challenge so effective. In the love of my parents, I must have detected the love of God who never abandons us no matter what sins we commit.

Sometimes we may feel the stakes are too high to remain silent, yet it *still* may be wiser to keep quiet. Perhaps we get a nagging feeling that it is morally necessary to tell loved ones when they are behaving badly. But frequently, even without words, others will know we disapprove of their behavior. It is not always necessary to verbalize our displeasure, and indeed that can be more harmful. Instead, showing love, rather than creating the impression that we approve, tells loved ones that despite our disapproval of the *behavior* we still approve of *them*. Sometimes, when those we love are engaged in sin, the most important thing they need to feel from us is our love and approval, not of what they do but who they are and who we know they can be.

Silence is powerful if we use it to surround statements of love and truth. However, if we always remain silent, our silence is impotent and weak. We must keep challenging or else we risk our silence becoming a silence of collusion. This is part of respecting our loved ones' freedom. Sharing our faith and challenging the behavior of those we love may be the only chance they receive to hear the truth in a culture that often tells them there is nothing wrong with their behavior. With God by our side, we can be open to inspirations to speak out and occasionally challenge in love. If we do this, we can be sure that even when our words are rejected or seem to be ignored, they will continue to resound powerfully in the minds of our loved ones.

Conclusion

"When he had spent everything."

— Luke 15:14

The prodigal son left his father's home, took his father's property, and "spent everything." In our culture, where many children leave home at age eighteen, this scenario is not quite as shocking as it would have been to people in the time of Jesus. But the prodigal son topped what was, in that time, the dishonor of leaving home and demanding his inheritance with the dishonor of wasting it. In ancient times this kind of behavior would have been unforgivable. However, it is very interesting to note the father's response to the son while he made very poor decisions.

Some Scripture translations say the son *"freely* spent everything." This translation emphasizes that the father did nothing to stop his son. The father would have been completely within his right to refuse the son his inheritance or at least to insist that the son stay in the vicinity of the family home so the father could keep an eye on him. The father does none of this. In fact, the father is conspicuously silent the entire time the son is behaving badly. The father's silent response to the son is not one of passivity, but of respect. The father does not respect his son's actions but his right to make free choices. Even though his choices are destructive and sinful, the father sees the hardness of his son's heart and knows that words will not be effective.

When we are involved in our sin and refuse to listen to God, or anyone else, he does not give up on us. Instead, God is at the window always waiting for us to return to his heart. But sometimes, like the father, God steps back, allowing us to exercise our free will, not because our choices are good for us, but because he respects our ability to make free decisions, good or bad. God is wise and knows when we make ourselves impervious to his guidance. But, at the right moments, God continues to make himself present in our lives, challenging us to change and, like the prodigal son, to come to our senses. In the same way, let us be humble, patient, ever forgiving, and strong like the Father. At times, we may have to raise our hands in surrender and, in respect for the free will of others, step away from interfering with their life choices. However, like the Father, we can continue to look for brief opportunities to encourage one another to pursue lives of true freedom.

Chapter Nine

Prayer Is Key

"Have confidence in prayer. It's an all-powerful gift that God has given us. Through it, you will obtain salvation for the dear souls that God has given you and all those you love." [1]

— Saint Peter Julian Eymard

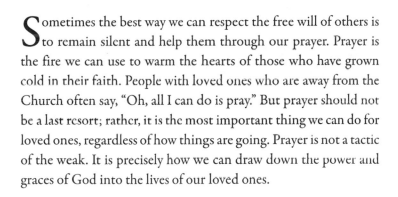

Sometimes the best way we can respect the free will of others is to remain silent and help them through our prayer. Prayer is the fire we can use to warm the hearts of those who have grown cold in their faith. People with loved ones who are away from the Church often say, "Oh, all I can do is pray." But prayer should not be a last resort; rather, it is the most important thing we can do for loved ones, regardless of how things are going. Prayer is not a tactic of the weak. It is precisely how we can draw down the power and graces of God into the lives of our loved ones.

Many converts say that the prayers of others were a major part of their conversion. Mike, a "revert" to the faith, relates how prayer played a part in his return to the Church:

As a teenager my addiction to alcohol, prescription drugs, and cocaine took me through several institutions and almost killed me. I spent every day working on ways to keep it going, like a demon above me with a hundred kicking feet. But all that time, God never left me. And neither did the prayers and tears of all the people in the Church who never failed in loving me.

Once during that time, I took part in a very drunken late-night conversation about religion. I was with a couple of artists, both heavy drug users. One of the fellows declared himself an agnostic, but held on to a vague faith in a cosmic life-force and some kind of continuance after death. He turned to his friend, who stated that he was an agnostic too, though more inclined to atheism. Holding his bottle, he then turned to me. "I'm a Christian," was my immediate and unexpected response.

I had no idea where that answer came from at the time and was even puzzled by it. I hadn't given so much as a moment's thought to God in years! But there, somewhere inside me, deeper than I could ever reach on my own, was something solid and unmoving, perhaps a "place" would be the best way to describe it. And that place extended far beyond any scrutiny or conviction on my part. It was deeper than human opinion.

Later in life, in prayer, I learned that this was the same place out of which my grandmother prayed for me while she was alive and in heaven after she had passed away. It was from this same place that my parents prayed when they saw me drugged and unconscious and still refused to give up hope. It was also the place from which the saints of the past and present embraced me in God. Though I'm often too immersed in the world to feel it, this is the place where my prayers arise from today. These aren't different places. It is one place, one world even, in Christ, where we all live and die. In that place I was never truly lost.

Like Mike, after my own conversion, I knew instinctively that my parents' prayers, the prayers of family and friends, and even the prayers of perfect strangers, on earth and in heaven, helped me to come back to the Church. This is an intuition that I cannot adequately explain, but I know it as much as I know that God exists. Sometimes, with great affection, I think of the anonymous strangers who knelt before God and asked him to bring me back to the sacraments. They did not know my name, they did not know my face, and yet they prayed for my salvation. I most likely will not meet them in this life, but I believe these strangers will be at the gates of heaven to greet me with joy, knowing that their prayers played a part in my conversion.

Prayer is *the* most important thing we can do for our loved ones who are away from the Church. It sounds trite. You have heard it before. But we cannot just know this intellectually; we need this truth to sink deeply into our bones and pervade our lives. Prayer is fruitful. The psalms tell us that "the Lord hears the needy" who call to him in their poverty and powerlessness (69:33). Prayer is also at the root of our spiritual life. If we do not pray, our relationship with God will wither away. We will lose perspective; we will be caught up in anxiety and fear; and we will drift away from God. The more we open ourselves to be nourished by God in our spiritual life, the more we will blossom, and the radiant beauty of our faith will draw others to the Church. When we pray, we tune into the presence of God in our soul. This is the most important thing that can happen for our loved ones. By becoming more like Christ through prayer, we will be able to invite our loved ones to the Church with the same tenderness and love of God, who so desires their salvation.

Our Prayers Make a Difference

Jesus makes it clear in Scripture that our prayers matter. One instance is particularly relevant to those who pray for loved ones whose faith is challenged. During the Last Supper, Jesus tells Peter: "Simon, Simon, listen! Satan has demanded to sift all of you like wheat, but I have prayed for you that your own faith may not fail; and you, when once you have turned back, strengthen your brothers" (Lk 22:31–32). In this passage, Jesus is not only encouraging Peter, he is also urging each one of us to pray for those whose faith is failing. If Jesus himself prayed for Peter, how much more should we pray for those we love when we see their faith faltering!

The words of Jesus, "when once you have turned back," are particularly revealing. They tell us that Peter turned away from Jesus, just as many of our loved ones turn away from his Church. It can be comforting to consider that even the first pope turned away from his faith in Jesus. Thankfully, Peter was not too far down the road before he heard the voice of Jesus calling him back. The ones we love may be quite far down the road, and some have seriously veered off the path. But Jesus teaches us in this Scripture passage that we can help them—with our prayers. Note that Jesus does not try to reason with or convince Peter not to betray him. Jesus does not waste his breath. He knows Peter's heart well. Peter is going to falter in his faith. So, Jesus chooses to pray for him.

The Lord's words in this passage are like a message in a bottle, thrown into the ocean of time. Jesus is talking to you and to anyone who is concerned about a loved one. He is telling us that prayer is the most important thing we can do for those who are faltering in their faith. Just as Peter turned back to Jesus, so our loved ones may also turn back. But we must have faith that our prayers are efficacious. Jesus himself tells us to have faith that prayer can make a difference, just as his prayer for Peter made a difference.

How Does Prayer Work?

Even if we believe in the power of prayer, it helps to understand why God saw fit to include prayer in the economy of salvation. After all, God can do anything—without the help of our prayers. He does not *need* our prayers. Nevertheless, as we have seen, Jesus clearly tells us in Scripture to pray and that our prayers are valuable. Why is this?

Saint Thomas Aquinas tells us that God "wishes to give us certain things upon our request"[2] because this strengthens our relationship with him. When God answers our prayers it helps us to trust him more and to praise him for all that he gives to us. If we did not need to pray, we would probably not recognize as many of the gifts of grace in our lives. Prayer helps us to remain aware of God's existence and thankful for the ways in which he provides for us and responds to our requests.

How much difference does prayer really make? C. S. Lewis tells us that God created us so that we would be able to make things happen both through physical action *and* spiritual action, or prayer. In other words, I can act in the physical world by opening a door. The door opens because I move my arm and push it open. Prayer works in a similar way. When we pray we are opening a door for grace. We can count on this reality, just like we can count on opening an unlocked door if we push it open. God tells us that if we ask for something, we will receive it. Of course, you might be wondering how praying can be like opening a door, because prayers are not always answered in the way we wish. But if everyone's prayers were answered in this manner, the world would be quite chaotic! Prayer is not like making a wish and rubbing a genie's bottle; it does not make us all-powerful like God. Rather, prayer entrusts our desires to God who will respond to them in the best way.

God has what C. S. Lewis describes as "discretionary power." We might say that God answers our prayers like a parent responding to a child's request. If your child asked to cross the street by herself, and you knew that a truck would be heading that way soon, you probably would not answer her request in the way she desired. God, like a good parent, has the power to use his discretion when answering our prayers. God sees the bigger picture beyond our requests, so he does not always respond to our prayers in the way we think he should. However, the power of God to exercise discretion when it comes to our prayers *does not weaken* the power of our prayers. If we pray for a loved one's return to the Church, we can be assured that our prayers are making a difference and that God is giving our loved one the grace necessary for his or her return. God may not answer our prayers in the way we think best, but nevertheless he always responds in the best way.

God always answers our prayers; he just takes our prayers and applies them in the best possible way. If we truly believe that our prayers are as powerful in the spiritual world as opening a door is in the material world, then we will be at peace. We can rest assured that even if it seems God is silent, it is because, in his perfect love, he is responding in a way that is best for us and for those we love, even if we cannot see immediate results in the material world.

We Are in This Together

You may recall the story in the Gospel of Mark about four men who had a paralyzed friend. The men's desire for their friend's healing was so great that they "removed the roof" of the house that Jesus was in and let their friend down through the hole they had made (2:4). The Gospel does not mention whether the paralytic man wanted to be lowered through the roof, but rather focuses on the initiative of his four friends. The Gospel says that "when Jesus saw their faith, he said to the paralytic, 'Son, your sins are forgiven'" (2:5). Jesus extends his graces to the man in the stretcher not because of this man's own faith, but because of the faith of his four loyal friends.

The story of the paralytic man should give us hope. Like the four friends, we are concerned about our loved ones, many of whom are paralyzed, maybe not physically, but by sin. While we cannot physically carry them to Jesus, in our concern we can bring them to God on the stretcher of our prayers. Jesus, seeing our faith, will give healing graces to our loved ones as he did for the paralyzed man. This Gospel story shows that our own faith can call down graces on our loved ones because faith connects us with others. At times, we are the ones on the stretcher, while the faith of others lifts us up to Jesus. We are a Church of faith, and joined together we can call down many graces on those who need them.

Scripture tells us that the early Christians "had all things in common" (Acts 2:44), which applies also to the reality of prayer in the communion of saints. The *Catechism* tells us that in the communion of saints, "the least of our acts done in charity redounds to the profit of all" (no. 953). As we pray for others who are faltering in their faith, we can be confident that the favor has been and will be returned. When our faith is weak, the prayers of others will raise us up. Even if we feel alone in our worry and prayer for our loved ones, we are not alone. Many others are praying with us. This is the beauty of Christian community—we lift our loved ones up in prayer, but we also pray for those we do not know who are in similar positions. Our prayers rise up to heaven and God responds to our prayers, spreading graces around to everyone, in the amount each one needs.

Conclusion

"But while he was still far off, his father saw him and was filled with compassion; he ran and put his arms around him and kissed him."

— Luke 15:20

The father spots the prodigal son returning while he is "still far off." Why does the father spot his son so quickly? Maybe it was because the father was scanning the horizon every day, waiting patiently and prayerfully for his son to return. The father did not send out a search party or go find his son himself and drag him home. No, the father knows that the most effective thing he can do for his son is not an outward action, but an inward stance of openness and prayer. The father sees a reality that is rich in the spiritual dimension. He knows that his prayers are powerful, perhaps more powerful than anything else he can do.

In the same way, we may see our loved ones, like the prodigal son, inhabiting a "distant country" of ideas and behaviors that seem so far removed from their true good (see Lk 15:13). We may feel like we need to do something; without action we feel impotent, powerless. But like the father, we are called to remember that prayer is active, a spiritual action. Although we may not see the results of our prayers, we can trust that God does. In the meantime, let us be open to our loved ones, to meet them while they are still "far off," and keep them in prayer even when things seem hopeless.

Chapter Ten

The Power of Suffering

"Suffering is the inner side of love."[1]

— Joseph Cardinal Ratzinger

———◇———

I remember the exact moment that I chose to become an atheist. It was not a moment of logic, but rather one of emotion, pain, and deep suffering. I was riding with my parents in the car one day when I was fourteen years old, my cheek pressed against the window. My father had recently lost his job under difficult circumstances, and my parents were struggling to pay the bills. I looked in the rearview mirror and could see my father was in a far-off place, his eyes full of concern. I could not understand how a loving, all-powerful God could allow my family to suffer like this, especially when my father had worked so hard for the

Church. I just could not reconcile a loving God with the suffering in my family and in the world. I reasoned that if God allowed this kind of suffering, then, even if he did exist, he might as well not exist to me.

The moment that thought crossed my mind, I claimed it as my own, and in that instant I became an atheist. The roots of my atheism did not lie in a logical refutation of the existence of God—that would come later. Rather than reasoning God's existence away, I simply denied it. I disowned God. Like a father who had let me down, I shut God completely out of my life. Your loved ones may also have a hard time believing in God because they have suffered greatly, perhaps because of the sins of other Christians. This is the negative power of suffering in many lives. Pain often causes people to push God away and even to deny his existence, because the thought of a loving God who allows terrible suffering can feel worse than not believing in God at all.

Of course, the simple answer to the problem of suffering is that the gift of free will necessarily brings evil into the world. God must allow evil in order for us to freely love him. Otherwise, without free will, our love for God would be coerced and meaningless, not real love. But easy answers do not relieve the pain that people experience when they suffer and feel that God is far from them. As Christians, we should try not to brush off difficult questions with answers that do not honor the confusion and pain that people experience. Suffering is truly a mystery, and to dismiss the hurt that people feel or to talk in platitudes will only seem false and naïve in a world filled with terrible pain. Rather, we are called to respond to the reality of suffering by living and reacting to it differently than the rest of the world. Suffering has the power to push people away from God, but, as Christians, we can live the message that God is powerful enough to bring good from whatever we experience.

When Jesus came to earth, he came to save us from our sin. Suffering remains in the world, but the death of Jesus helps us to understand its meaning more clearly. Jesus came to show us the face of the Father, a revelation that culminated in his death on the cross. God chose to reveal himself most profoundly in the very act of suffering. Jesus chose to suffer for us, although he was more innocent than any other victim of suffering and was in no way connected to the inheritance of original sin. In this selfless act, Jesus redeemed and transformed suffering with his love. Suffering is not inherently meaningful, but Jesus gives it meaning and value by taking it upon himself. If we recognize the spiritual value in suffering, we can approach our own suffering and the suffering of others in a way that is both compassionate and helpful.

Suffering in Scripture

Jesus makes it clear in Scripture that suffering is a necessary part of the Christian life. After all, he regularly said such things as, "If any want to become my followers, let them deny themselves and take up their cross daily and follow me" (Lk 9:23). But understanding the meaning of Christian suffering does not come naturally to us. We have been conditioned to believe that our goal in life should be to escape suffering, embrace convenience, and live in uninterrupted contentment. Among some Christian denominations, the idea that God punishes us with suffering and rewards us with health and wealth is unfortunately alive and well. All of this, along with original sin that presses upon us to look out for ourselves, avoid suffering, and seek pleasure, creates deep confusion in our hearts about the meaning of suffering.

When evil entered the world, suffering entered too. This is made clear when God sends Adam and Eve away from the Garden of Eden. He says to Eve, "in pain you shall bring forth children," and to Adam, "by the sweat of your face you shall eat bread until you return to the ground" (Gn 3:16, 19). Because they chose to disobey God, to separate themselves from their loving Creator, Adam and Eve also chose to suffer. So the first book of the Bible links suffering to sin. With the poison of sin, suffering comes as its effect. We might say, "Well, that's not fair; we weren't in the Garden of Eden, we didn't choose to eat the fruit." That's certainly true; we did not eat the fruit of the Tree of the Knowledge of Good and Evil. However, it is also undoubtedly true that we all participate in sin and choose to separate ourselves from God. And, upon reflection, most of us will admit that given the chance in the Garden of Eden, we most likely would have eaten the forbidden fruit as well. So, in some sense, the evil of suffering is linked to our own sin, whether we like it or not.

The people of the Old Testament understood well that sin was linked to suffering. However, they incorrectly assumed that when people suffered it was their own fault. They believed a person's suffering was directly linked to one's own personal sin or the sins of one's ancestors. This is why in the Book of Job—after Job loses his home, his wealth, and his family—Job's friend Bildad tells him that his suffering must be due to some kind of sin on his part. Bildad challenges Job with the question: "Does God pervert justice?" (8:3). If God is a God of justice, Bildad reasons, then surely he would not allow an innocent person to suffer. This reasoning sounds legitimate, but in the Book of Job, God makes it clear that suffering is not subject to justice in the world. The suffering that humans experience is often unjust. Job, a righteous man, suffered. Suffering, therefore, is not given to us in proportion to our sin. In fact, if we look at reality, the most defenseless and innocent often suffer more than others.

In his ministry, Jesus encountered confusion about the connection between suffering and sin. In one instance, people ask him about the "Galileans whose blood Pilate had mingled with their sacrifices" (Lk 13:1). This brutal killing on the Temple grounds must have shaken people, and they wondered if the suffering experienced was deserved. So Jesus responds with a question: "Do you think that because these Galileans suffered in this way they were worse sinners than all other Galileans?" (13:2) Jesus answers his own question with a forceful, "No, I tell you . . ." (13:5). In these few words, Jesus teaches a very important lesson about suffering. Though linked to sin, suffering is not necessarily proportionate to personal sin. The Galileans who suffered at the hands of Pilate did not do so because they were more sinful than other people. But Jesus does not pretend that these men were completely innocent either. He acknowledges that although they were not "*worse* sinners" than others, they were still sinners. By this, Jesus affirms that the universal source of suffering is sin, whether we experience it because of our own sin, the sins of others, or indirectly through original sin.

Then Jesus teaches us a second lesson by linking suffering to an exhortation to repentance. He continues, "But unless you repent, you will all perish just as they did" (13:5). With these words, Jesus points out that the ultimate suffering is to perish without repentance for sin and to experience eternal separation from God. This second message is perhaps one of the most important ones Jesus teaches us about suffering, not only in this scenario but with the lesson of the cross. In order to avoid eternal suffering, the worst suffering possible, we must repent and live good lives. Sometimes we become so involved in the suffering of the here and now that we lose an eternal perspective. But Jesus reorients us. By doing this, he does not diminish the suffering experienced here on earth. Rather, he points out that terrible earthly suffering, though at times appalling, is finite. No matter how horrific a person's suffering may be, eternal suffering is always worse than a suffering with a beginning and an end.

As Jesus continued his ministry, he kept on teaching about suffering. He made it clear to his disciples that even he, the Son of God, would undergo serious suffering. He often spoke of his imminent, violent death. In one memorable passage, Jesus tells the disciples that when they arrive in Jerusalem, he will be condemned to death and people "will mock him, and spit upon him, and flog him, and kill him; and after three days he will rise again" (Mk 10:34). The apostles James and John, consumed with thoughts of their own honor, respond to this heart-wrenching revelation by asking Jesus if they can sit at his right and left hand. We often respond similarly when Jesus shows us that the cross is part of the Christian life. We ignore him and expect an earthly reward for our good behavior. Many of us subconsciously expect to be given a pass from suffering for trying to live a good Christian life. Unfortunately, this attitude often leads to shock and a refusal to accept suffering when it comes. We do not realize that by embracing our daily crosses we embrace Jesus, and in this our reward is far greater.

Suffering and Redemption

All of this positive talk about suffering may have you feeling a bit uncomfortable. This is pretty normal. Aside from paper cuts and such small bothers, real suffering is not easily accepted, let alone embraced. On a human level, Jesus himself did not welcome the extreme suffering of the cross. In the Gospel of Matthew he prays, "My Father, if it is possible, let this cup pass from me; yet not what I want but what you want" (26:39). In this exchange between our heavenly Father and his Son, we recognize the pain that many of us experience when we suffer. We know that God, being all-powerful, could take away our suffering. Yet, he usually does not choose to do so. Why? Because when he allows suffering, God is always powerful enough to bring about a greater good. For Jesus, it was the redemption of the human race.

For us, God allows evil and suffering so that we may have free will. With the dangerous gift of free will inevitably comes sin, and with sin comes suffering and great evil. But God, in his mercy and abundant love, does not simply tolerate suffering in order to give us free will. Instead, God used the evil of suffering to bring about the greatest good in the world, our redemption from sin. Through his Son's death, God lifted up the human reality of suffering, transformed it, and filled it with salvific grace. The very reality of suffering has been made different by the cross. In his apostolic letter *On the Christian Meaning of Human Suffering* (*Salvifici Doloris*), Saint John Paul II wrote: "*To suffer* means to become particularly *susceptible*, particularly *open to the working of the salvific powers of God*, offered to humanity in Christ."[2] This means that if we suffer in union with the suffering of Jesus, we have special access to the graces that the death and resurrection of Jesus provide for us. This new reality allows us to unite ourselves to Jesus in our suffering and as a result draw down graces for ourselves and the world.

We may intellectually understand the connection between the suffering of Jesus and our redemption from sin. However, it is usually more difficult for us to believe that suffering has the potential to play a positive role in our lives on an individual level. When we are in the midst of suffering, it can be hard to believe that it can positively change and transform us. It might help to think of a life devoid of suffering, like a father who feeds his child sweets from morning to night. This may be what the child desires, but it is not good for her; it does not help her grow and become healthy. In the same way, our human nature, wounded as it is by original sin, needs to be trained to understand what is good for it. The normal, daily suffering—and even out-of-the-ordinary suffering—we endure can be like the vegetables that make a child grimace but are ultimately good for her to eat. Our heavenly Father knows what is good for us, and we can trust that although he may not will our suffering, he can use it for our good.

The Anesthesia of Our Divine Physician

An excerpt from *A Story of a Soul* by Saint Thérèse of Lisieux can help us understand how God uses suffering as an opportunity for grace in our lives. In this classic work, she describes how she feels about falling asleep during prayer:

> That I fall asleep so often during meditation, and thanksgiving after Communion, should distress me. Well, I am not distressed. I reflect that little children are equally dear to their parents whether they are asleep or awake; that, in order to perform operations, doctors put their patients to sleep.[3]

This image of God putting us to sleep so he can work on something within us is applicable not only to falling asleep in prayer, but also to what God does within us when we undergo a painful experience.

When we suffer something acutely, we may feel as if we have been pushed into another dimension. We are aware of the world in a different way; it is as if everything vibrates with the intensity of our pain. We may feel more detached, but also very much alive at the same time. I compare this feeling to a spiritual anesthesia. God allows us to be taken out of normal existence to experience something that numbs us to the core. This numbing is an opportunity for God to enter our lives with his scalpel of love and to work on issues in our spiritual life when we otherwise would not have been open to it. Of course, God does not force his expertise on us. Like a good doctor, he needs the cooperation of his patients. Cooperation in the spiritual realm does not necessarily mean consciously assenting to God's work in us, but it does mean opening ourselves to God in our distress, even if only with a silent call for help.

Periods of intense suffering usually end, and we go back to living our normal lives. However, the lessons learned when we were more open to the scalpel of the Divine Physician stay with us. We may feel that we quickly forget these lessons, but in reality, if we are open to it, God's work in us is something we can build upon in the future so as to become less and less self-centered. God does not necessarily will the painful things we experience in order for this to happen. Suffering most often happens because we live in an imperfect, sinful world. But if we are open, our loving God uses these times as opportunities for intense change in our spiritual lives. We can reject these opportunities for transformation and resist the suffering. But we are going to suffer anyway. Why not suffer with Jesus and become a person positively transformed by our suffering?

Suffering for Our Loved Ones

Individual transformation is one positive aspect of suffering. Our own personal transformation through suffering can help our loved ones. When we allow God, the Divine Physician, to use everything in our life for good, including suffering, then we become more holy. Our own spiritual transformation and holiness will draw our loved ones to the faith. But another aspect of suffering, even more relevant to our loved ones' spiritual journeys, is redemptive suffering, our ability to draw down graces for our loved ones through our sufferings. Rather than spending all our energy fighting and resisting inevitable suffering, when we embrace it, we draw down graces from heaven for souls who need them, including our loved ones.

Saint Paul writes: "I am now rejoicing in my sufferings for your sake, and in my flesh I am completing what is lacking in Christ's afflictions for the sake of his body, that is, the church" (Col 1:24). At first read, this Scripture passage can be confusing. How could anything be "lacking" in the suffering of Jesus? However, Paul's words make sense in light of redemptive suffering. God has "left room" for our contribution to his own redemptive suffering, so that we could participate in the power of his redemption. He does this not because he needs us to participate in his salvific action but because he wants to give us this precious opportunity, in our small and humble way, to become more Christ-like and help others.

Often, we associate redemptive suffering with serious, terrible pain that people experience in unusual circumstances. And, certainly, when we endure extraordinary pain, we have an opportunity to offer it up for those we love. Suffering is a special kind of offering because through it we participate in a special way in the sacrifice of Jesus on Calvary. But we do not have to wait for a terrible illness or injury; every moment is an opportunity to draw down graces for our loved ones. We know from the countless examples of the saints that we can offer up virtually anything to Jesus, and he has the power to transform it for the good.

What we offer up to God for our loved ones does not have to be huge; the offer just has to be sincere. Saint Thérèse tells us: "Pick up a pin from a motive of love, and you may thereby convert a soul."[4] We can offer up the smallest things, and they make a difference. If someone's manner of talking irritates us, we can offer up our irritation to the Lord and ask that it help someone else. If we do not feel like getting up early, we can offer our sacrifice for the sake of someone who we know needs help. If we do not like to eat green beans, we can offer up our displeasure at eating them for someone else's sake. We can even offer up the moments of joy in our lives in thanksgiving to God for all that he has done for us and for our loved ones. What we can offer will almost always be small, we are only human. But God loves humility. Like a mother who delights in her children's handmade gifts, God delights in our little offerings, and he rewards them more generously that we can possibly imagine.

Another beautiful opportunity to participate in the redemptive power of the cross comes to us in the Mass. A friend once shared with me one way we can participate in the Eucharistic celebration. At the consecration, when the priest raises the paten with the host, we can mentally place our loved ones on the paten and offer them to God as well. In this offering, we entrust our loved ones to God's loving mercy. It is a small gesture, but one that God surely honors and treasures. When we participate in the Mass we can join our offering to the offering Jesus made for our sins. The Mass is like a doorway that allows us to enter the moment in time when Jesus gave everything for us. In the Mass, this most important moment in history becomes timeless, stretching through the centuries; it becomes a moment in which we can participate on behalf of our loved ones, interceding for them and all of humanity.

When Our Loved Ones Suffer

Suffering for others probably comes more easily to us than watching our loved ones suffer. If we are lucky, we can ease a loved one's suffering by lending a helping hand or saying an encouraging word. But it is particularly difficult to watch others suffer when we can do nothing to help them. It can be heartrending when we are forced to step back from a loved one's suffering, but we can do this in the faith that God is at work in the lives of those we love and that our prayers for them are powerful.

In order for us to be at peace in these moments, it is important to pray for the grace to trust in God. Whether the suffering is willed or simply allowed by God, we can be sure that he can and will use it as an opportunity and a vehicle for his grace. Accepting our own pain and the pain of others is a signal to God that we trust him. It shows that we are open to the work he is ready to do through the suffering in our lives and those of our loved ones. Drawing the most beauty and grace from our own inevitable suffering and the suffering of others ultimately depends on trust. Do we trust God enough to believe he can bring good from suffering, even the worst suffering in the world?

On a human level, we may long for our loved ones not to suffer. However, especially if they are making bad decisions, we can be sure that some of these choices will have natural consequences that cause suffering. A life that seeks to escape suffering often finds itself face-to-face with deep agony, ironically precisely as a result of attempts to avoid it. We see this in the lives of people who become addicted to drugs or who are involved in serial relationships searching for companionship and security. When these situations occur in the lives of those we love, we should certainly try to help as much as possible. But sometimes we can only pray and allow others to suffer while we seemingly sit by, unable to do anything else to help them.

So often we feel helpless when we watch our loved ones suffer from the choices they make. However, this helplessness does not necessarily mean inactivity. We can ask for the grace that our sorrow resemble the powerful sorrow of Mary at the foot of the cross. Gerald Vann, OP, gives us a beautiful picture of the active sorrow of Mary:

> [Mary] saw through the anguish and helplessness of death, the renewal of life; through the savage winter, the coming of the spring. She saw, but more than that, she hastened its coming by the silence and stillness of her sorrow.[5]

When we are able to suffer as Mary, quietly and peacefully, then our suffering becomes helpful to those around us, a silent prayer that hastens a resolution to the suffering we want so much to alleviate. In the end, we are called to trust, like Mary, that God can forge a path to himself through our loved one's suffering. Like the sacrifice of Jesus, the suffering in our lives and in the lives of others can be a conduit of grace for ourselves, our loved ones, and the whole world.

Conclusion

> "He would gladly have filled himself with the pods that the pigs were eating; and no one gave him anything."
>
> — Luke 15:16

The prodigal son cuts himself off from his father, wastes his riches, and then finds himself physically and spiritually empty. The son has stooped so low that he begins to envy the pigs he tends. Even so, in the midst of his misery "no one gave him anything" (Lk 15:16). The father, who may have heard news of him or assumed that his son would end up in dire straits, does not look for him or send rent checks. The father's mercy is not a mercy of "false kindness" that enables bad behavior. No, the father knows and accepts the positive change that suffering can bring about in his son. It is painful to see our loved ones suffer, but suffering is inevitable in life, especially in a life away from God. Yet as Christians, we are called to view suffering in light of eternal life. Our loved ones may experience great pain, but we can live in the trust that God will ultimately use their suffering for good; it may be exactly what pushes them back to the Father's house.

Because of the cross, suffering is now on our side. Our suffering can be offered to God as a source of grace for transformation in another person's life. The father, seeing his son's bad decisions, must have felt the same pain in his own heart that we feel now when we think of our loved ones. This pain, in addition to other things we can offer up, can be entrusted to the Father who will use it for our loved ones' redemption. The pain of our hearts joins the pain that God feels when he sees our friends and family, his own sons and daughters, straying from his merciful heart. In the light of the cross of Jesus Christ, suffering has become a pathway for all to the Father. The Father watches this pathway carefully, and at the first sign of our loved ones' change of heart, he will come running to them with arms wide open.

CHAPTER ELEVEN

Be Saints, It Is All That Matters

"The meaning of life is to be a saint."[1]

— Peter Kreeft

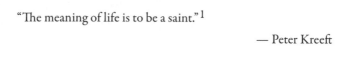

My grandma, Elinor Brandi Shea, was a woman who enjoyed life. My grandfather, Charles Shea, died young, leaving her to care for five children on her meager salary as secretary at the local Catholic school. Despite the tough circumstances of her life, or perhaps because of them, my grandmother was a strong and holy woman. I got to know her because every time one of my four younger siblings was born, Grandma Shea would get on a plane and spend a couple of weeks helping my mom around the house. When she would visit, we would play endless card games. She never tired of me asking to play, but I do not remember ever winning one game against her. When I would complain, she would say to me, "Theresa, life won't give you a break, so I don't give you a break. You have to win fair and square."

I don't remember discussing God with my grandma, but her life spoke to me of God. Sometimes the holiest people are not those who flaunt their faith or talk about pious things, but rather those who live their lives to the fullest, loving everyone around them. Elinor Shea was this kind of holy—she loved me, she loved my family, she loved everyone, and her love spoke of God. It was not hard for her to love because she lived life to the fullest. She suffered. She lived through tough times. But in her Catholic faith she found the strength to persevere. She was one of those rare persons who grow and mature to the fullest capacity of their humanness. Like a bonfire amid candles, her wisdom and strength shone brightly on those around her.

The Evangelization of Attraction

Sometimes when loved ones leave the faith, we think we need to *do* something. But effective evangelization is really less about doing and more about *being*. My Grandma Shea preached her faith by being herself, by exuding warmth, strength, maturity, and joy. God calls us to holiness more than he calls us to the work of evangelization. Holiness is primary. Why? Because more than anything else, holiness attracts others to the Church. Pope Francis affirmed this when, echoing the words of Benedict XVI, he wrote: "It is not by proselytizing that the Church grows, but 'by attraction.'"[2] Evangelization is more about attraction than it is about anything else. When we have loved ones who are away from the Church, God asks us to become holy so that we may give glory to God and attract others to him in the Church. In short, God asks of us the same thing he asks regardless of our situation—to become saints.

The sentiments of Kate, a fallen away Catholic, demonstrate why it is important for us to be holy:

> I'm really into female saints that I learned about when I was a child, like the story of Saint Maria Goretti (which my mother taught me; she was very impacted by it, that someone could have such total faith and abandonment in the most horrific of moments). Padre Pio is adored as a major force in my family's religious beliefs and personal prayers. I believe absolutely and definitely in these people, but find it hard to say, "I believe in God."

Kate's feelings are understandable; it is hard to believe in a person who lived 2,000 years ago if we see no evidence of Jesus still alive today. But that is why our holy example can be the substance, or the evidence, that others need to make a step in faith. If a person does not know God, it is through other human beings that he or she will come to know him. We each are the dwelling place of the Trinity through our Baptism, and we are called to be the evidence of the continuing presence of Jesus in the world. The Church is the Body of Christ on earth. Our loved ones may find it difficult to believe in God, and unfortunately many Christians make it even more difficult due to unloving behavior. However, when we truly experience God's love through another, it is hard to deny that God exists.

By becoming pure conduits of God's love, we draw others into a love relationship with the Trinity. This is our calling in life. This is the most important mission that God gives us. Being a saint is not for the "special" or "unique." It is not about doing something amazing. It is simply about loving God, and loving him above everything else. It is not only for self-disciplined ascetics and brilliant theologians. Being a saint is for me. It is for you. It is for everyone. As Saint John Paul II put it once: "God created us to share in his very own life. . . . He calls us to be his: he wants us all to be saints."[3]

What, you may ask, does all this have to do with our loved ones who are away from the Church? It has everything to do with them. If we are honest with ourselves, we know that our sin is a barrier to proclaiming the Gospel, the good news of God's love for the world. We try our best to give good example, but we often do not model God's love to our spouse, children, friends, and neighbors. Let's be honest with ourselves: *we* are the reason there are not more Christians in the world. The Body of Christ is filled with weak, fallible human beings who, by sinning, work against the very mission of the Church all the time. This is not to make anyone feel guilty, which would be completely unhelpful. God does not want us to wallow in guilt. Rather, when we feel like everything outside of us is out of our control, it helps to focus on the one thing over which we do have some control: our will to become a saint. The more our behavior conforms to that of Jesus, the more likely we are to attract others to God. This is the simple truth. Be a saint. It is the best thing we can do to bring others to Christ.

Surrendering to the Transformation

If you are like me, you feel exhausted just thinking about the prospect of trying to be a saint. We often lump becoming a saint with other difficult goals in life. To become a concert pianist, I must work hard, take lessons, and practice for hours. I listen to classical music and study music theory. I have the power to do all of these things, and whether or not I do them is really up to me. Becoming a saint, however, differs a bit from becoming a concert pianist. I say it differs a bit because it is not totally different.

Becoming a saint does require the will to become one. It also requires passion and time. But the good news is that becoming a saint is not as much something that *we* work on as something *God* works on. We just have to let him.

We may believe that becoming a saint requires abundant activity. We feel we need to engage in many private devotions, acts of mercy, and exterior actions. These things are certainly good in themselves, but they will not make us saints. Adding activity upon activity, no matter how pious, will not magically transform us into saints. Rather, it is in *surrendering* our activity to God that we will become holy. Often we are afraid to do this because as much as we love God, deep down we believe that God will be much too hard on us. Little do we know, we are often much harder on ourselves than God would ever be. Regardless, we can count on the fact that life will be much harder when we choose not to walk it with God.

For good reason Jesus tells us in the Gospels to take up his yoke, for it is easy and light (see Mt 11:30). A yoke has room for two oxen. When Jesus tells us to take his yoke, he is telling us that he is going to walk with us. As humans, we often think that doing things on our own will be easier. We have a tainted concept of freedom, and, to a certain extent, all of us believe life will be easier if we go about our business without consulting God. But the truth is that we are going to carry a yoke either way. Life is hard, and we make it even harder when we do not accept God's help and direction. It's just common sense to carry our yoke with Jesus, and not only to let him help when things get rough, but also to let him lead.

Surrendering to God's lead is a moment-by-moment activity. We cannot say, "I have surrendered myself to God, that's done with!" Rather, surrender is much like a love relationship. Spouses know that loving one another requires daily affirmation of their love. In the same way, surrendering requires daily effort. Even more, it requires moment-by-moment effort. Because we are human and very weak, we find it difficult to let go of our firm grasp on our lives. We are addicted to control, and escaping this addiction requires constant, daily work.

Saints of Small Things

Josemaría Escrivá once wrote: "Great holiness consists in carrying out the 'little duties' of each moment. Great souls pay much attention to little things."[4] Being a saint is not as much about huge heroic decisions as it is about making small decisions throughout our day in union with Jesus. We can do very little to show our love for God, and even the very little we do causes us great sacrifice because we are so weak. When someone puts me down or disagrees sharply with something I have said, it takes everything inside of me not to hold a grudge or retort sarcastically. But when I look inside myself, ask for God's help, and respond rightly, I know that God uses these moments to make me holier. God knows our weakness. And rather than spurning our paltry offering, he accepts it and rewards it with the grace we need to become saints.

On the cross, Jesus suffered from the pain of lashes on his back, nails in his hands and feet, sores and injuries all over his body, and because he was hanging on the cross, he had to struggle to breathe. In the throes of this pain, he said, "I am thirsty" (Jn 19:28). Mother Teresa's life was centered on these words. She taught her sisters that they revealed God's intense desire for our love. The soldiers responded in much the same way we respond to God's thirst for our love, by giving him what is sometimes translated as "common wine" (19:29). Jesus must have known, when he said, "I thirst," that he would be given either nothing or something less than satisfying. Yet, he said it all the same. Often, all we can give Jesus is the "common wine" of our love, expressed in the smallest of things. But Jesus accepts it. He not only accepts it, he thirsts for it.

When we do even the smallest things for love of God, whether it be not eating a piece of chocolate we crave, or resisting the urge to be sarcastic, or even picking up a small piece of trash from the ground when no one is looking, all of these things are precious in the eyes of God. He not only pours out graces on our loved ones when we offer these things to him, but he also uses these moments to transform our common wine into the best of wines. Just as at the Wedding of Cana, Jesus changes the plain, simple, and unsatisfying nature of our human love into something that is pure, sweet, and refreshing—the best wine available. God fills us with the wine of his love: a wine that is beautiful and attractive, a wine that will draw those around us to him.

Union with God

Making sacrifices for others and surrendering to God's work in our soul may still seem like an overwhelming task. But we can be at peace. Being a saint is not about anxiously trying to make every sacrifice possible or beating ourselves up when failures to surrender to God's will inevitably occur. Sanctity is not about perfection, exteriorly at least. This is impossible. When Jesus urges us to "be perfect, therefore, as your heavenly Father is perfect," he urges us to *participate* in the perfect wholeness and holiness of God (Mt 5:48). Participate is the key word here. We are not capable of being God. But we can *participate* in God's perfect holiness when we unite ourselves to him so that he may love through us.

Union with the Trinity will make each of us a saint. All I have written about before, such as surrendering to God and making sacrifices for our loved ones, is possible only if we unite ourselves to God. The humanity of Jesus is like an extension cord that plugs into the powerhouse of God. Jesus has already made the connection. We are hooked up to this connection; we are united to God through our Baptism. Now, in order to become saints, we need only to tap into the power of God's indwelling within us. When we cannot love, when we cannot forgive, when we cannot follow Jesus's commandment to love our neighbor as ourselves, we can ask God, living right within us, to love through us, to forgive through us, to shine through us. Pope Francis makes it clear that union with God is essential to our Christian life:

> Being Christian is not just obeying orders but means being in Christ, thinking like him, acting like him, loving like him; it means letting him take possession of our life and change it, transform it, and free it from the darkness of evil and sin.[5]

When we live in Jesus, his holiness begins to act from within us, attracting others to God through our closeness to him.

Conclusion

> "Quickly, bring out a robe—the best one—and put it on him; put a ring on his finger and sandals on his feet."
>
> — Luke 15:22

Why aren't more of us saints? It's not because God does not want to give graces to the brave people who ask for them, but because so few ask. It is so hard for us to believe in God's generosity. Even when, like the father of the prodigal son, God embraces us in our imperfection and sin and calls for the best robe and puts a ring on our finger, we still draw back. We doubt we can really be saints. We think we will just let God and ourselves down. We underestimate who God made us to be. Like the elder son who stands outside of his father's house refusing to come in, we refuse God's graces, we refuse his entreaties. We doubt the Father's insistent words, "All that is mine is yours" (Lk 15:31).

We convince ourselves, saying, "Surely he doesn't mean me. That robe and ring must be for someone else—extraordinary Mother Teresa types—not me." We think that sainthood is too difficult, too painful. We do not trust God enough to believe that, though difficult, the path to sanctity is a path to true happiness, not just in heaven but on earth, right here, right now. We just need to believe that God only wants the best for us, but we do not trust him! The Father is waiting; he has a ring and the best robe in his arms, and he is waiting for us to accept them. He waits for our assent, our trust not in ourselves but in him and in his love for us.

The Father's love for us is urgent, not only because he deeply cares for us but also because he created us to give glory to him through our lives, to draw others to God through our holiness. There are a lot of evangelism tactics out there, many effective and good, but none of them compare to personal sanctity. What could be more effective in drawing others to God than God himself living within us, acting within us, and shining from within us? The prodigal son returned to the father precisely because he knew that his father would have compassion on him: "I will get up and go to my father, and I will say to him, 'Father, I have sinned against heaven and before you; I am no longer worthy to be called your son; treat me like one of your hired hands'" (15:18–19). The father cared for his servants, so the son knew he would care for him; his compassion was evident. The father's love was like a magnet, drawing his son back home. In the same way, when we become like the Father, when we let the Father act in us and through us, our loved ones will be drawn to the powerful love of God present in our lives.

CHAPTER TWELVE

Becoming a Person of Hope

"If we love until it hurts, God will give us his peace and joy." [1]

— Mother Teresa of Calcutta

———◇———

W hen I was in high school, I knew a girl who left the faith around the same time I did. Her mother lit candles, prayed, had Masses offered, and talked to her about God and the faith whenever she could. Several years later I was shocked to hear from my friend, who was still not practicing the faith, that her mother had stopped going to church. I was confused. Her mom had been so faithful. She loved God with all her heart. It just did not make sense to me. Later, after meeting my friend's mom and asking her what had happened, I realized that her prayers for her daughter and for her other children who had left the faith had worn her out. She had not seen any progress, and with little support from her husband or family, she had felt alone. So she gave up. She left the Church so she could let go of a situation that was hurting her deeply.

Sometimes, when our loved ones make bad choices, we resort to unhealthy behaviors. On the one hand, when a situation seems hopeless and causes us too much distress, we may retreat into indifference. "It is your life," we say, throwing up our hands in surrender. We may cease praying for that person. Our loved ones' loss of faith can drive us to feelings of sadness and doubt. In some cases, as with my friend's mother, we may even give up our own practice of the faith. Temptations to abandon faith can surface in our loneliness and anguish. However, giving up our own practice of the faith, while temporarily distracting us from our feelings, ultimately leads to greater despair and will only make it more likely that our loved ones will not return to the Church.

In whatever form it takes, indifference is understandable. It is a form of self-protection. We cannot endure the pain of seeing our loved ones abandon God or the Church, so we try to convince ourselves that it does not matter. We may pretend the faith is not important, or we may simply give up on our loved ones. When we face the possibility that someone we love may never return to the Church, it can cause us great sadness that we want to avoid. This is even more the case if we feel any sort of responsibility for that person's actions. However, God wants to help us. No matter what we have done or said, our loved ones' decisions to leave the Church are their own. God wants us to live our faith first for him, not for our loved ones. As important as they are, to you and to God, we can draw others to God only if we put our own faith lives first.

On the other hand, if we tend to the opposite extreme of being too involved, this is just as damaging to ourselves and others. When we lose ourselves in our emotions, we end up feeling constantly burdened and fearful. To end the pain, we may resort to trying to control our loved ones. We nag, act aggressively, or shut them out of our lives in an attempt to force them to change. One mother once confided in me that she told her son over and over again that he would go to hell because he had left the faith. She told me this without the slightest inkling that it might not be a good idea to repeatedly say something like that. When we live in anxiety and hopelessness, we act in ways that make it even less likely that others will consider exploring the faith again. When we speak from our own self-centered fear, rather than from love, we often end up pushing others further away.

Both of these extremes are two sides of the same coin. In fact, most people, like the mother of my high school friend, often exhibit one extreme only to resort to the opposite when the first tactic doesn't work. Both of these behaviors are a result of losing hope. They come from a heart that loves more than it can handle; a love that becomes heavy and too painful to endure. We try to end the pain by rejecting the person or the faith that is the source of our hurt, or we try to force our loved ones to see things our way. It is important to recognize and accept that none of these approaches will bring our loved ones back to the Church. The extremes of apathy and caring too much not only don't work, they repel others. However, in the practice of hope, we need not fear extremes; we can hope as much as we want.

Saint Thomas Aquinas insists that "hope has no mean or extremes . . . since it is impossible to trust too much in the Divine assistance."[2] If we tend to gravitate toward extremes, it is best to gravitate toward extreme hope, for excessive hope will not harm our relationship with our loved ones. Those we love will see the light of Christ only in a person of hope. We do not necessarily hope for our loved ones to return to the Church because it is reasonable to hope for this or because we see signs that what we hope for might happen. We hope because we believe. Our hope has a name and it is Jesus. Our loved ones may disappoint us, cause us great sadness, and drive us to feelings of despair, but all these feelings vanish in the burning light of hope. Like the legendary vampire that flees from light, our dark emotions cannot stand side by side with our hope.

No matter how weak this virtue feels, it is always greater than darkness because hope is rooted in God. In Psalm 62, the psalmist confirms this reality: "For God alone my soul waits in silence, for my hope is from him" (v. 5). And Saint Paul tells us that God not only gives us our hope but that he *is* a God of hope and our hope is strengthened by the Holy Spirit: "May the God of hope fill you with all joy and peace in believing, so that you may abound in hope by the power of the Holy Spirit" (Rom 15:13). The Scriptures tell us that faith and hope go together. When we have faith in God, we let God inhabit our lives and transform us. With God's help we can become a people whose hope shines for all to see and whose lives attract others to God.

Nothing Is Impossible with God

We hope not because we have the power within ourselves to do so but because we are participating in a long line of faithful who, stretching through the centuries, have put their hope not in created things but in God. We are a Church of hope. Abraham, our father in the faith, "hoping against hope" believed that God would give him many descendants (Rom 4:18). Hannah hoped for a son and God granted her request with her son Samuel. The entire nation of Israel hoped for a Savior and God gave them more than what they hoped for: his only Son. We hope because we have seen the hope of our ancestors in the faith, and we know that, just as he was there for them, God will be there for us. Even in the darkest of places God does not disappoint.

The greatest story of hope in Scripture and in humanity is found in the event of the annunciation, when the angel Gabriel appeared to Mary and told her:

> "You will conceive in your womb and bear a son, and you will name him Jesus. He will be great, and will be called the Son of the Most High, and the Lord God will give to him the throne of his ancestor David. He will reign over the house of Jacob forever, and of his kingdom there will be no end." (Lk 1:31–33)

We know the story so well that we often do not stop to consider the miraculous response Mary gave to the angel.

In order to highlight the astonishing nature of Mary's response, the evangelist Luke contrasts her reply with Zechariah's response to the angel's message that he and his wife Elizabeth will bear a son: "'How will I know that this is so? For I am an old man, and my wife is getting on in years'" (1:18). Pope Benedict XVI observed that, unlike Zechariah, Mary "asks not whether, but how" the angel's message will be fulfilled: "How can this be, since I am a virgin?" (1:34) In other words, Mary is so full of faith that, unlike Zechariah, she does not stubbornly distrust the possibility of what the angel tells her. Benedict continues: "Mary appears as a fearless woman, one who remains composed even in the presence of something utterly unprecedented."[3] Mary is not completely shocked by the angel's message because she is a woman of remarkable faith. Even though she must have felt overwhelmed that God would choose to work through her in such a way, she responds with one clarifying question, and then surrenders herself with joy to God's will.

In this moment of the annunciation, Mary reveals herself as a woman of hope. The *Catechism* describes hope as "placing our trust in Christ's promises and relying not on our own strength, but on the help of the grace of the Holy Spirit" (no. 1817). This is exactly what Mary did; she trusted the angel Gabriel's message: "The Holy Spirit will come upon you, and the power of the Most High will overshadow you" (1:35). Mary trusted Gabriel's words because she trusted God and believed that he could do great things. This was not an isolated moment in Mary's life. She believed the angel's message and submitted to it because all of her life she had cultivated a disposition of hope and trust in the Lord. For Mary, the annunciation was the culmination of a life of hope-filled assents to the will of God.

If we hope, we follow Mary's example of trust in the Lord, knowing that he can do great things in the lives of those we love. God is a God of the impossible. If we cannot bring ourselves to believe this, then we know that we have become too separated from Mary's way of viewing the world: a way full of hope, expectation, and trust.

Reason to Hope

I often tell people whose loved ones are inactive Catholics that I was once away from the Church. I assume it is because I am now in religious life and passionate about the faith, but my confession is often met with disbelief and a look from the person that suggests he or she thinks that I merely missed Mass once or twice. These people cannot seem to believe that someone who was once away from the Church for over ten years would now be in religious life. This reaction signals to me the need for many faithful to regain an ambitious sense of hope for their loved ones.

If, at the darkest times in my life, someone had told me that I would not only return to the Church but enter religious life, I probably would have told them they should check themselves into a psychiatric hospital. I did not believe in God, so surprises of this kind were completely out of the question. Life was in my hands and no one else's, so how could that ever happen? But as believers, we are called to move beyond such jaded attitudes. As Christians, we can live in the hope of someone who knows a God beyond all understanding. No matter how gloomy the situation, God can do great things in our lives and in the lives of others, things which are far beyond our understanding.

The perfect example of this is found in the central mystery of our faith, the cross. Atheists often have very negative reactions to the idea of a religion centered around a God who died on a cross. It baffles and even infuriates them that someone would see something good in that terrible scenario. To the eyes of one who recognizes only physical, material reality, the cross is gruesome, sadistic, and strange. But we know, through faith, that although we live in a three-dimensional world, many more spiritual dimensions exist, and God sees them all. God helps us to see how an outwardly appalling situation can actually be miraculous. In the midst of suffering, violence, and pain, God brought about his greatest act of love and mercy. This helps us have hope that God is at work in the situations where we least expect him to be, sometimes even more so.

Practical Tips to Grow in Hope

Hope is a virtue, so we can grow in hope just as we can grow in faith and charity. Growing in virtue is not easy; it requires patience, determination, and good will. But with God's help, we can become more hopeful people. In the *First Letter of Saint John*, we are told that "God is light and in him there is no darkness at all" (1:5).

Being a believer means we are people of the light, people of God. When we are in the darkness of hopelessness or indifference, we are not living in the presence of God; instead we are turned inward on ourselves. Hope cannot be found within ourselves, we must turn to God in order to grow in this virtue. As Pope Benedict XVI wrote in his encyclical *Saved in Hope* (*Spe Salvi*): "Let us put it very simply: man needs God, otherwise he remains without hope."[4] With that in mind, here are some ways we can practice the virtue of hope.

Practice Charity

The virtues are interconnected so when we practice one virtue, it lifts up another. In this case, when we practice concrete acts of charity for others our hearts grow in hope. Pope Francis points out that hope grows "from the joyful and practical exercise of the love,"[5] that we ourselves have received from God. The use of the word "practical" is vital here. We cannot carry out acts of charity while daydreaming on our living room couches. We need to get up and act; we can do this inside of the home with our own family and communities, but we can also extend the circle of our charity to people we don't know, people who are strangers but part of our human family. Stretching our hearts in charity will stretch our capacity to hope.

Hope in Prayer

Pope Benedict XVI described prayer as a "school of hope."[6] We learn hope in prayer because we grow closer to God who is the source of our hope. We cannot expect to think like God if we do not give him time to change our thinking. When we pray, we usually find it easy to unburden ourselves before God, but too often we do this and then think our prayer time is over when in fact it has just begun! In speaking to God, we also need to stop and listen. This gives God an opportunity to connect with us and teach us how to see things differently. Encountering God in prayer helps us to grow in hope, to see our situation and the situations of others more clearly in the light of God's love and mercy and the power of grace.

Practice Reverence

Saint Thomas Aquinas relates the virtues to the gifts of the Holy Spirit. The virtue that corresponds to hope is fear of the Lord. When we fear the Lord we do not cower in terror or fear of punishment. Father Raniero Cantalamessa, OFM, puts it this way:

> Fearing God is different from being afraid. It is a component of faith: It is born from knowledge of who God is. It is the same sentiment that we feel before some great spectacle of nature. It is feeling small before something that is immense; it is stupor, marvel mixed with admiration.[7]

We can grow in this reverence for God through simple activities. We can go hiking or just get outside to experience the power of God through nature. We can adore God especially in Eucharistic adoration, acknowledging his glory face to face. We can also grow in fear of the Lord through the sacrament of Reconciliation or Confession, in which we own and accept our weakness before the goodness of God. The more we get to know God, the more we will fear hurting him. We begin to trust in his power more than ourselves. This humble attitude leads us to grow in the virtue of hope.

Examples of Living Hope

We can also grow in the hope that our loved ones may return to the Church through conversion stories that inspire. These stories remind us of what is possible and help us to look upon our loved ones' lives with hope and love. Saint Paul is a great example of conversion in Scripture. Before he became Paul, he was known as Saul, a zealous Jew. Some might say, "Well, at least he was religious!" But Paul was a fanatic, so much so that he justified extreme violence against Jews who followed Jesus. Paul's conversion has become such a staple of our faith that we forget how extreme his behavior was. He was a murderer! As the apostle Stephen was stoned, Saul looked on—with delight one assumes— while people laid their cloaks before him, a sign that Saul was most likely the instigator of Stephen's death. And yet, in the life of a man gone so far astray, God intervened. At the least likely moment, while Paul was on his way to persecute more Christians, Jesus appeared to him.

This encounter radically centers Paul on Jesus, changing his life completely. Paul writes of this change, "I persecuted the church of God. But by the grace of God I am what I am" (1 Cor 15:9–10). Paul's encounter with Jesus on the road to Damascus was pure grace that allowed him to change. If we think of the trajectory of Paul's life like a transcontinental plane on route from North America to Asia, the change that occurred at the moment Jesus appears to him is equivalent to an Asia-bound plane beginning to fly vertically to Mars. This is how fundamentally an encounter with Christ can change a person's life. This encounter can happen over many years or it can happen in a moment. We see more of these life-changing events throughout Scripture. The wise men, upon leaving Bethlehem after seeing the baby Jesus, "left for their own country by another road" (Mt 2:12). Why would the Gospel writer tell us this small detail if not to indicate something that is spiritually true as well? An encounter with God knocks people off course; lives and plans change when we meet the person of Jesus.

We can find evidence of this reality in our own time and place, in books, radio shows, and even in the people around us. Anthony, a young man from California, has an unforgettable story of return:

> I came back to my Catholic faith in prison. When I was nineteen years old, I was sentenced to sixty-three months in federal prison for a drug trafficking charge. When I first entered the correctional system I was not ready for a genuine change. While in prison, I continued living the same lifestyle that got me there in the first place.
>
> My conversion began one night while I was smoking meth and looking at a dirty magazine. Right then I felt in my heart that I had to change my ways; after all, I was engaging in the very same behaviors in prison as the ones that had led me there in the first place. The Holy Spirit came to me when I was at my lowest point. At that moment I knew God was calling me to himself.
>
> It is up to the individual person and the grace of God to open their hearts and receive the good news. But the defining moment for me happened during a "meth fueled epiphany," crazy but true. I felt the Holy Spirit at that moment with power and conviction. The next Saturday I heard over the loud speaker that Catholic Mass would be held in five minutes in the prison chapel. Though I hadn't been to church in years, I felt in my soul that I had to go.

Beautiful stories like these are a testament to the miraculous mercy of God. If we saw someone like Anthony in prison, smoking meth and looking at dirty magazines, we probably would not even try to get through to him. "He is too far gone," we might say to ourselves. But God is not like us. He is always near to us, no matter what we do, and he tries to enter our hearts at every moment, sometimes even more so at the least likely of times. We can rest assured when our loved ones' situations seem hopeless, God has not given up. He is whispering gently into their ears, constantly calling them back to him.

Even when our loved ones make choices that seem irrevocable and ominous, we know from Scripture, the lives of the saints, and from modern conversion stories, that one encounter with Jesus can drastically change the worrisome trajectory of a person's life. Jesus gradually prepares us for encounters with him, encounters that will transform us. Every situation is an opportunity for grace. This is the miracle of God's revelation to us in the world. A healthy spiritual life is marked by change. Sometimes the change is a drastic showstopper like Paul's; at other times it involves more subtle movements in the soul. As we strive to continually live in conversion and allow God's grace to change us, we pray that our loved ones will become more open to the transformative power of God's action in their own lives.

Realistically, we know that every story will not have the ending that we desire. Some of our loved ones may never return to the Church. But this reality is not a reason to lose hope or to lose our own faith. As Saint Paul wrote: "We know that all things work together for good for those who love God" (Rom 8:28). God is so powerful that he can bring good from *everything*, even when his beloved children leave the Church or reject him completely. In the end, our hope remains firmly rooted in God, knowing that the salvation of our loved ones is in his powerful hands. Even if those we love die of an overdose, suicide, or in a moment of serious sin, we know that God is merciful and he can work out their salvation in the short moments before they draw their last breath. Our hope lies not on a natural level of reasoning but transcends the natural and is lifted on the wings of faith to reside in the heart of our omnipotent God of hope.

Conclusion

"This son of mine was dead."

— Luke 15:24

In the parable of the Prodigal Son, the father acknowledges that when his son was apart from him, he was dead. These words of the father upon his son's return reveal the depth of his suffering when his son cut himself off from him. It is clear, however, that in the midst of his great suffering, the father maintained hope. This is evident in the father's steadfast patience. The father doesn't seem greatly surprised or shocked by his son's return. The son does not walk in on a meal or find his father busy with some household task. No, it seems that the father had been hopefully looking out for his son, his eyes fixed on the path upon which his son might return. The father was so attentive, so hopeful, that he was able to see his son approach "while he was still far off" (Lk 15:20).

What does the father's hopeful waiting stance reveal for us in our lives? While we may be tempted to leave our vigil by the window and give up, to either forget our loved ones and write them off or chase after them with emotional pleas, we are called to be like the father who waited hopefully for his son. Our hope is our future joy. Without hope, the father may have been surprised or ambivalent upon his son's return, but his overflowing joy reveals the patient hope that he nourished while his son was away. Saint Paul reveals this connection between hope and joy in the Letter to the Romans: "Rejoice in hope, be patient in suffering, persevere in prayer" (12:12). We can rejoice in our hope even before it is fulfilled because our hope is rooted not in the future, but in God. We can rejoice in God, who is the source of goodness, hope, and all that is cause for rejoicing. We know God. We are in relationship with God. And it is from him that we find our motivation to continue in hopeful, joyful relationship with our loved ones.

Epilogue

"The gaze of Jesus always makes us worthy, gives us dignity. It is a generous look."[1]

— Pope Francis

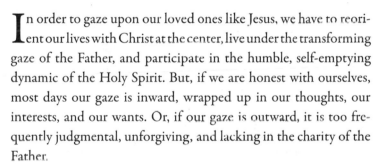

In order to gaze upon our loved ones like Jesus, we have to reorient our lives with Christ at the center, live under the transforming gaze of the Father, and participate in the humble, self-emptying dynamic of the Holy Spirit. But, if we are honest with ourselves, most days our gaze is inward, wrapped up in our thoughts, our interests, and our wants. Or, if our gaze is outward, it is too frequently judgmental, unforgiving, and lacking in the charity of the Father.

It is not easy to model our lives after Jesus, to remain in communion with the Father, and to respond to the invitations of the Spirit. But this is the life of love, the work of holiness, and the path of joy for which we were made. A life of continual transformation allows us to become more and more like Jesus, who desires to inhabit our lives to such an extent that when we look upon our loved ones, we look upon them with the eyes of Jesus. It is these eyes that will attract our loved ones to the Church; it is this gaze that will tenderly transform and lead them to the Father. Such an approach to life will not be easy, but it is our path to heaven so that, with our loved ones, we may together "gaze on the beauty of the LORD" (Ps 27:4, NIV).

As we continue to strive to look upon our loved ones with God's tender gaze of transforming love, let us live under the gaze of the Father, fix our eyes upon Jesus, and be guided in love by the Holy Spirit.

Appendix

Prayers

———◇◇◇———

Prayer to the Holy Spirit

Holy Spirit, your very breath is an invitation to grace. Its sweetness fills the lives of those who open their souls to your love. So many ignore you, hate you, spit on you, and refuse your presence in their lives. But you remain with them, breathing an invitation to joy, serenity, and peace.

Pour out your graces on me and on my loved ones who are away from the Church. Help me to pray as I ought, to say the words you want me to say, to do what you want me to do, and to love with your love. Help me to inspire, to encourage, to walk with, to support, and to challenge. But help me to do all this wrapped only in your love.

Holy Spirit, free me from my anxiety, my anger, and any despair that I might feel. I know none of this is from you. You fill me only with peace and trust. Continue to fill me with faith that all can work together for good, even when all—to my weak, faithless eyes—looks hopeless.

Breathe into the lives of all who are far from you. Help my loved ones to accept your invitation to breathe the air of grace, the air that transforms, renews, and revitalizes.

Breathe into my own life, which needs your inspiration, your gentleness, and your peace. Please give me the strength and the courage I need to be your presence in others' lives.

Be with me and those I love, this day and all days.

Prayer to Jesus

Jesus, sometimes I feel such sadness when I see my loved ones reject your presence in the Church. I long for them to see, to understand, and to delight in your Presence in the Eucharist. I desire the same joy and grace for them that I have found in the sacraments.

Yet, for reasons I cannot understand, my loved ones do not accept your presence in the Church. This causes me great suffering, but I know that it causes you greater suffering. Despite the pain that I feel, I am grateful for my suffering, which I know is a participation in your love for humanity, in your thirst for souls.

In faith I join the suffering I feel to the suffering that you experienced on the cross. On the cross you bore the rejection of all sinners, including me. I undergo this suffering willingly, knowing that I cause you suffering with my own sin and rejection of you in my own life. I offer this sacrifice up to you with joy and with love, knowing that you will use my sacrifice for great good.

Prayer for Conversion

Dearest Jesus, I offer you my heart. Transform it, so that it may be more like yours. I want to be your presence to those far from the Church, but so many things hold me back: my fear, my sin, my weakness. Jesus, work through all these things every day, to make me more like you. I entrust all this to you in faith and love, dear Jesus. Be with me and my loved ones.

Prayer to the Trinity

Blessed Trinity, I have faith that you dwell within me through my Baptism. I ask that you fill me with your presence. May your divine presence permeate my actions, my words, and my life. May you be the air I breathe, the space I inhabit, and the time I live in.

I long for my loved ones to experience your presence in their souls, fed by the grace of the sacraments. Every time I reorient myself to your presence within my soul, I offer my loved ones to you as well. May you reorient their lives to be centered in you. May they discover the joy it is to live continually in your presence.

Prayer to Saint Monica

Saint Monica, the mother of Saint Augustine, prayed for her son even when it seemed that he was very far from God and had left the faith for good. Her prayers were rewarded, and Augustine not only returned to the Church but became a saint and doctor of the Church. God rewards our prayers, our hope, and our faith-filled longing that our loved ones may experience the fullness of the love of God in the Church. The words of Saint Monica recorded by Saint Augustine give us hope in this reality:

"Son, for myself I have no longer any pleasure in anything in this life. Now that my hopes in this world are satisfied, I do not know what more I want here or why I am here. There was indeed one thing for which I wished to tarry a little in this life, and that was that I might see you a Catholic Christian before I died. My God hath answered this more than abundantly, so that I see you now made his servant and spurning all earthly happiness. What more am I to do here?"[1]

Saint Monica, in the most hopeless of circumstances you trusted God; you prayed even when it seemed that your prayers were useless. Please help me continue to hope and pray for my loved ones. Please intercede for me on their behalf and pray that God will reward my prayers with an abundance of grace as he did for you.

I particularly place *(Name)* before you. Please pray for *(Name)* with the same fervor and love for which you prayed for your own son Augustine. I beg you to bring the name of my loved one before God in heaven and ask him to pour his graces into his/her life.

Prayer to Saint Augustine

Saint Augustine, your heart was restless until it rested in God. Please intercede for *(Name)*; ask God to help him/her to feel the restlessness of heart you felt and to search with openness and humility for the only One who can satisfy our longing. You know better than anyone what it is to be lost. Help all who have gone astray find their way back home, to the Church.

Prayer to Venerable Matt Talbot for an Addict

Gentle Matt Talbot, intercede for my friends and family who are controlled by addictions to drugs and alcohol that keep them far from God. Keep my loved one, *(Name)*, particularly in your prayers. You know the struggle it is to leave behind addiction. You know how difficult it is to have a relationship with God when something else becomes the obsessive center of a person's life. Ask God that he may give an abundance of grace to those who struggle with addiction, especially *(Name)* whom I love so much. May God give him/her the grace to leave addiction behind and return to Jesus in the Catholic Church.

Morning Offering for Fallen Away Catholics

God, I offer to you the sufferings, sacrifices, and even the joys of this day for all souls who have wandered from your Church and from the flowing font of graces in the sacraments. Please help these souls to feel the emptiness of a life without the grace of the sacraments. Lead them to your healing power in the Eucharist and in the sacrament of Confession. May the souls of all who have wandered from the Church rediscover the renewing and transformative power of your love, present in the sacraments.

A Prayer for Conversion

Thank you, Father, for you created all of us to be your children, to be united to you, to be with you. Just as an earthly father longs to hold, guide, guard, and love his child, so do you long to hold us close to you. Lord, we pray for all those who do not know your love, who have never felt your embrace. Lord, may their hearts be opened to allow you to embrace them and to grow in the desire to embrace you in return. May their hearts be opened to allow you to know them, their darkness and their joy, and to fill them with your light, truth, peace, and healing. Lord, we pray for the conversion of all your children. May you be our joy, our fulfillment, our love, our life. Through your grace, may we become the people that you made us to be, and may we join together to offer you a bouquet of roses, a bouquet of our souls.

by Erin Nolan

Lead Them, Lord . . .

(Based on the parable of the Prodigal Son, Luke 15:11–32)

Lord Jesus, hear my prayer and answer me.
See my aching heart and come to my aid.
Give me your heart to wait patiently,
to wait patiently for my loved ones' return to you.
Show them the way to you; show them the Father
that they may steer away from a life of dissipation.
What pastures are they feeding on, Lord?
What waters are giving them life?
Lord, be close to them and do not abandon them.
Let them feel you close and not despair;
through your gentle hand, lead and guide them.
To you who are the everlasting Way.
Amen.

by Sr. Jacqueline Jean-Marie Gitonga, FSP

Mother, You Know . . .

O Mother fair, O Mother dear,
see your child in these moments of despair.
As I groan, and search for ways
to bring back into your arms my beloved ones,
you who love them more than I,
you who see their steps and strides,
take my anguish, my longings, and grant me peace.
Knowing that you love them much more than I,
give me the words to say to them, the gestures of love,
that through me you may reach out and lead them
    to your Son.
Help me, dear Mother, help me I pray.
Use me as you wish and in whichever way.
Amen.

by Sr. Jacqueline Jean-Marie Gitonga, FSP

To Saint Paul, Lover of Souls

O Saint Paul, athirst for all souls,
see my beloved ones, gone astray.
Nothing is impossible for God.
Help me to see this, and to believe.
Reach out to them, and bring them to the fold,
scattered here and there in this world so cold.
Bring them back so that the life of Christ may
once again flow through them, in them and in me.
Amen.

by Sr. Jacqueline Jean-Marie Gitonga, FSP

A Personal Act of Contrition

Lord, Jesus Christ, you gave your life for me that I may be consoled by your presence here on earth and one day be with you in heaven. I thank you for your merciful love. When I have sinned, let my heart break with sorrow in order to find my way back to you. When I am weak and faced with temptation and my past sins flash through my mind, I find it hard to forgive myself even when I know you have forgiven me. I am unworthy of the Father's love, yet you desire to enter my heart and restore my dignity. Teach me to love like you. Help me to forgive those who have hurt me so that I too may accept the Father's mercy with my whole heart, mind, and strength. How else can I love you in my weakness but to fall down on my knees and allow you to embrace me? I want to love you for the rest of my days and to become holy, to glorify you, and to bring others to your love. From now on, may my life glorify your name. Amen.

by Sr. Khristina Galema, FSP

Jesus, I Feel Helpless

Lord, often I encounter people who have left the Church. Some of them have been badly hurt. Others are indifferent. Others have just put their faith on the back burner and haven't made their relationship with you a priority. In general, it's not too hard to be compassionate, to take them where they are at, to realize that they are on a journey, to offer them a word to ponder and then entrust it all to you. But when it comes to my family, Lord, and those whom I deeply love, this "letting go" and trusting is so much harder and I feel so helpless. I want them to be happy. I want them to find you, and I wish you could break into their hearts now. Jesus, I offer you my helplessness and my utter dependence on you. I believe that your love for those I love is so much greater than mine, and that in your time your love will break through in a gentle way that respects their freedom. Jesus, please help me to serenely embrace my helplessness and to continually turn to you with trust. I believe that you will make everything beautiful in its time (see Eccl 3:11).

by Sr. Carmen Christi Pompei, FSP

February 2015
Dear Zsaa,
Happy Birthday!
Love & Prayers always,
Chix

Notes

———— ⬦⬦ ————

Introduction

1. Antonio Spadaro. *La Civiltà Cattolica*, "Wake up the World: Conversation with Pope Francis about the Religious Life," translated by Donald Maldari, accessed January 13, 2014, http://www.laciviltacattolica.it/articoli_download/extra/Wake_up_the_world.pdf.

Chapter Two

1. Saint Augustine, Lib. de Salut. xxxii.

2. Pope Francis, *Lumen Fidei* (*Light of Faith*) (Boston: Pauline Books & Media, 2013), no.14.

3. Blaise Pascal, *Thoughts*, translated by W. F. Trotter, Vol. XLVIII, Part 1, The Harvard Classics (New York: P.F. Collier & Son, 1909–14), Bartleby.com, 2001, www.bartleby.com/48/1/.

4. Saint Athanasius, *De inc.* 54, 3: PG 25, 192B.

5. See Saint Thomas Aquinas, *Summa Theologiae*, II-II, q. 161, a. 5.

Chapter Three

1. Hans Urs von Balthasar, *Heart of the World* (San Francisco: Ignatius Press, 1980), 91.

2. Jacques Philippe, *In the School of the Holy Spirit* (New Rochelle: Scepter Publishers, 2007), 45.

3. See Pope John Paul II, "Holy Mass at the Cathedral of St. Matthew Homily of His Holiness John Paul II, Washington, October 6, 1979," accessed January 9, 2014, http://www.vatican.va/holy_father/john_paul_ii/homilies/1979/documents/hf_jp-ii_hom_19791006_washington-san-matteo_en.html.

Chapter Four

1. Pope John Paul II, "Homily of John Paul II for the Canonization of Edith Stein," accessed April 2, 2014, no. 6, http://www.vatican.va/holy_father/john_paul_ii/homilies/1998/documents/hf_jp-ii_hom_11101998_stein_en.html.

2. Pope Benedict XVI, *Charity in Truth (Caritas in Veritate)* (Boston: Pauline Books & Media, 2009), no. 1.

Chapter Five

1. G. K. Chesterton, *Collected Works of G. K. Chesterton,* Bk. 35 (San Francisco: Ignatius Press, 1992), 293.

2. Joseph Cardinal Ratzinger, "Mass 'Pro Eligendo Romano Pontifice' Homily of His Eminence Cardinal Joseph Ratzinger, Dean of the College of Cardinals, April 19, 2005," accessed January 10, 2014, http://www.vatican.va/gpII/documents/homily-pro-eligendo-pontifice_20050418_en.html.

3. Saint Augustine, "Letters of Saint Augustine: Letter 211 (A.D. 423)," from *Nicene and Post-Nicene Fathers, First Series,* Vol. 1, edited by Philip Schaff and translated by J. G. Cunningham. Accessed January 10, 2014, http://www.ccel.org/ccel/schaff/npnf101.txt.

4. Pope John Paul II, *Redemptoris Missio (Mission of the Redeemer)* (Boston: Pauline Books & Media, 1991), no. 9.

5. Second Vatican Coucil, *On the Relation of the Church to Non-Christian Religions (Nostra Aetate)*, no. 2, http://www.vatican.va/archive/hist_councils/ii_vatican_council/documents/vat-ii_decl_19651028_nostra-aetate_en.html.

6. It is important to note that the Catholic Church shares valid sacraments and apostolic succession with many ecclesial communities in the East. Many of our Christian brothers and sisters of other faiths share some of our views on the importance of sacramental life, particularly Baptism. The *Catechism* states: "Those 'who believe in Christ and have been properly baptized are put in a certain, although imperfect, communion with the Catholic Church.' With the Orthodox Churches, this communion is so profound 'that it lacks little to attain the fullness that would permit a common celebration of the Lord's Eucharist'" (*CCC* 838). This is relevant insofar as the closer our loved ones get to the true sacramental life that God intended, the closer they are to communion with the Catholic Church.

7. Second Vatican Council, Dogmatic Constitution on the Church, *Lumen Gentium* (Boston: Pauline Books & Media: 1965), no. 11.

8. Pope Francis, *Joy of the Gospel (Evangelii Gaudium)* (Boston: Pauline Books & Media, 2013), no. 99.

9. Ibid., no. 139.

10. Ibid., no. 85.

Chapter Six

1. Tomáš Halík, *Patience with God: The Story of Zacchaeus Continuing in Us* (New York: Random House, 2009), 35.

2. Saint Augustine, Sermo 52, 6, 16: PL 38, 360 and Sermo 117, 3, 5: PL 38, 663.

3. Marc Barnes, January 6, 2011, Bad Catholic blog entry "Doubt," accessed January 10, 2014, http://www.patheos.com/blogs/badcatholic/2011/01/doubt.html.

4. Saint Gregory the Great, *Office of Readings*, "From a homily on the Gospels" (Boston: St. Paul Editions, 1983), 1462.

Chapter Seven

1. Pope Francis, "Solemnity of Pentecost, Holy Mass with The Ecclesial Movements: Homily of Pope Francis Saint Peter's Square Sunday, May 19, 2013," no. 2.

2. Pope Francis, *Joy of the Gospel*, no. 112.

3. Saint John Chrysostom, *The Catecheses* (Cat. 3, 13–19; SC 50, 174–177).

4. T. Douglas Murray, ed., *Jeanne d'Arc: Maid of Orleans, Deliverer of France; being the story of her life, her achievements, and her death, as attested on Oath and Set forth in the Original Documents* (New York: McClure, Phillips & Co., 1902) Six Public, Examinations,18.

5. *Lumen Gentium*, no. 8.

6. Pope Paul VI, *On Evangelization in the Modern World (Evangelii Nuntiandi)* (Boston: Pauline Books & Media: 1976), no. 80.

7. Pope Francis, *Joy of the Gospel*, no. 6.

8. Ibid., no. 15.

9. See Thayer and Smith, "Greek Lexicon entry for Ousia," The NAS New Testament Greek Lexicon, 1999, http://www.biblestudytools.com/lexicons/greek/nas/ousia.html.

Chapter Eight

1. Hans Urs von Balthasar, *Heart of the World* (San Francisco: Ignatius Press, 1980), 142.

2. Pope Paul VI, *On Evangelization in the Modern World*, no. 14.

3. Pope Francis, *Joy of the Gospel*, no. 8.

4. Archbishop George H. Niederauer, "Archbishop's Journal—Free Will, Conscience, and Moral Choice: What Catholics Believe," *Catholic San Francisco*, January 13, 2010, accessed January 3, 2014, http://www.catholic-sf.org/news_select.php?id=56744.

5. *Pope: Gospel Must Be Preached Gently, with Fraternity and Love*, *Zenit*, January 3, 2014, accessed January 3, 2014, http://www.zenit.org/

en/articles/pope-gospel-must-be-preached-gently-with-fraternity-and-love.

6. Pope John Paul II, *Mission of the Redeemer*, no. 39.

Chapter Nine

1. Peter Julian Eymard, From a letter written on January 4, 1864 to Mme. Mathilde Giraud-Jordan, "Je vous remercie de vos vœux," accessed January 11, 2014, http://www.eymard.org/eym/sr.asp?Init=1. Author translation.

2. Thomas Aquinas, *Summa Theologiae*, II–II, q. 83, a. 2.

Chapter Ten

1. Joseph Cardinal Ratzinger, *God and the World: A Conversation with Peter Seewald* (San Francisco: Ignatius Press, 2002), 323.

2. Pope John Paul II, *On the Christian Meaning of Human Suffering (Salvifici Doloris)* (Boston: Pauline Books & Media, 1984), no. 23.

3. Thérèse Martin, *The Story of a Soul (L'Histoire d'une Âme): The Autobiography of St. Thérèse of Lisieux with Additional Writings and Sayings of St. Thérèse,* translated by Thomas Taylor and edited by Rev. T.N. Taylor, (London: Burns, Oates & Washbourne, 1912; 8th ed., 1922), http://www.gutenberg.org/cache/epub/16772/pg16772.html.

4. Ibid.

5. Gerald Vann, OP, *The Pain of Christ and the Sorrow of God* (New York: Alba House, 1993), 50.

Chapter Eleven

1. Peter Kreeft, *Catholic Christianity: A Complete Catechism of Catholic Beliefs Based on the Catechism of the Catholic Church* (San Francisco: Ignatius Press, 2001), 89.

2. Pope Francis, *Joy of the Gospel*, no. 15.

3. Pope John Paul II, "Message of the Holy Father to the Youth of the World on the Occasion of the 15th World Youth Day, June 29, 1999,"

no. 5, http://www.vatican.va/holy_father/john_paul_ii/messages/youth/documents/hf_jp-ii_mes_29061999_xv-world-youth-day_en.html.

4. Josemaría Escrivá, *The Way,* nos. 817, 818, accessed January 7, 2014, http://www.escrivaworks.org/book/the_way-contents-39.htm.

5. Pope Francis, *General Audience,* April 10, 2013, http://www.vatican.va/holy_father/francesco/audiences/2013/documents/papa-francesco_20130410_udienza-generale_en.html.

Chapter Twelve

1. Mother Teresa of Calcutta, *Come Be My Light: The Private Writings of the "Saint of Calcutta,"* edited by Brian Kolodiejchuk (New York: Doubleday, 2007), 146. [Mother Teresa's words to co-workers, March 1, 1995.]

2. Thomas Aquinas, *Summa Theologiae,* II–II, q. 17, a. 5.

3. Pope Benedict XVI, *Jesus of Nazareth: The Infancy Narratives* (New York: Random House, 2012), 33–34.

4. Pope Benedict XVI, *Saved in Hope (Spe Salvi)* (Boston: Pauline Books & Media, 2007), no. 23.

5. Pope Francis, *Joy of the Gospel,* no. 142.

6. Pope Benedict XVI, *Saved in Hope,* no. 32.

7. Raniero Cantalamessa, "Have Fear But Do Not Be Afraid: Gospel Commentary for 12th Sunday in Ordinary Time," translated by Joseph G. Trabbi, *Zenit,* June 20, 2008, accessed January 8, 2014, http://www.zenit.org/en/articles/have-fear-but-do-not-be-afraid.

Epilogue

1. "Pope Francis at Mass: the merciful gaze of Jesus," Official Vatican Network, September 21, 2013, accessed January 18, 2014, http://www.news.va/en/news/pope-francis-at-mass-the-merciful-gaze-of-jesus.

Appendix

1. Saint Augustine, *Confessions and Enchiridion*, translated and edited by Albert C. Outler (Philadelphia: Westminster Press, 1955), accessed February 3, 2014, http://www.ccel.org/ccel/augustine/confessions.txt.

BOOKS & MEDIA

The Daughters of St. Paul operate book and media centers at the following addresses. Visit, call, or write the one nearest you today, or find us at www.pauline.org.

CALIFORNIA

3908 Sepulveda Blvd, Culver City, CA 90230	310-397-8676
935 Brewster Avenue, Redwood City, CA 94063	650-369-4230
5945 Balboa Avenue, San Diego, CA 92111	858-565-9181

FLORIDA

145 S.W. 107th Avenue, Miami, FL 33174	305-559-6715

HAWAII

1143 Bishop Street, Honolulu, HI 96813	808-521-2731

ILLINOIS

172 North Michigan Avenue, Chicago, IL 60601	312-346-4228

LOUISIANA

4403 Veterans Memorial Blvd, Metairie, LA 70006	504-887-7631

MASSACHUSETTS

885 Providence Hwy, Dedham, MA 02026	781-326-5385

MISSOURI

9804 Watson Road, St. Louis, MO 63126	314-965-3512

NEW YORK

64 W. 38th Street, New York, NY 10018	212-754-1110

SOUTH CAROLINA

243 King Street, Charleston, SC 29401	843-577-0175

TEXAS

Currently no book center; for parish exhibits or outreach evangelization, contact: 210–488–4123 or SanAntonio@paulinemedia.com

VIRGINIA

1025 King Street, Alexandria, VA 22314	703-549-3806

CANADA

3022 Dufferin Street, Toronto, ON M6B 3T5	416-781-9131

¡También somos su fuente para libros,
videos y música en español!